River of Memory

The Everlasting Columbia

River of Memory
The Everlasting Columbia

William D. Layman

Wenatchee Valley Museum & Cultural Center Wenatchee, Washington
in association with
University of Washington Press Seattle / London
UBC Press Vancouver / Toronto

Dedicated to Salmon who have nourished land and people,
and to all of the indigenous bands, tribes and nations
who have drawn strength from the river.

This publication was made possible in part by a grant from the Joan Paterson Kerr Fund.

© 2006 by the Wenatchee Valley Museum & Cultural Center

"Where Winter Burbot Roil" and "Somewhere in the Heavens" © 2006 by Peter Christensen

Printed in China
Design and composition by William D. Layman
12 11 10 09 08 07 06   5 4 3 2 1

Published simultaneously in the United States and Canada

University of Washington Press
P.O. Box 50096, Seattle, WA 98145-5096
www.washington.edu/uwpress

UBC Press
The University of British Columbia
2029 West Mall, Vancouver, B.C. V6T 1Z2
www.ubcpress.ca

Cataloging-in-Publication Data can be found at the back of the book.

The paper used in this publication meets the minimum requirements of American National Standard for Information Sciences— Permanence of Paper for Printed Library Materials, ANSI Z39.48–1984.

Cover Photograph: Salmon Jumping Lower Kettle Falls, Ellis Morigeau, William Teakle Collection, Northwest Room, Spokane Public Library.

Back Cover Photographs (Top to Bottom): Cascade Rapids, Carleton E. Watkins, Oregon Historical Society, OrHi 2108; Kettle Falls, William Teakle Collection, Northwest Room, Spokane Public Library; Near Canyon Creek, British Columbia Archives, D-02829.

Inset: Entrance of the Columbia from Astoria Looking West, Steven Lehl Collection.

The Wenatchee Valley Museum & Cultural Center gratefully acknowledges major funding support from:

The Murdock Charitable Trust (Vancouver, WA) and
The Icicle Fund (Leavenworth, WA)

Additional sponsorship and support by
American West Steamboat Company
Chelan County PUD
Douglas County PUD
Humanities Washington
Harold and Margaret Weed
Community Foundation of North Central Washington

Published in conjunction with the exhibition
River of Memory: The Everlasting Columbia
William Layman, guest curator, and Terri White, co-curator

Exhibit Venues

Wenatchee Valley Museum & Cultural Center
Wenatchee, Washington   April 21 through December 31, 2006

Washington State History Museum
Tacoma, Washington   January 15 through April 15, 2007

Touchstones Nelson: Museum of Art and History
Nelson, British Columbia   May 5 through August 5, 2007

Northwest Museum of Arts & Culture
Spokane, Washington   August 26, 2007, through January 7, 2008

Royal British Columbia Museum
Victoria, British Columbia   February 1 through April 30, 2008

Tamástslikt Cultural Institute
Pendleton, Oregon   May 22 through September 27, 2008

Contents

Lower Cascade Rapids

Albert Henry Barnes, 1913   University of Washington Libraries, Special Collections, Barnes 1589

Foreword

The Columbia River has shaped the landscape, natural history, culture, and economy of the Pacific Northwest since time immemorial. In every manner imaginable, the Columbia River, celebrated in songs, poems, histories, legends, and myth, is the lifeblood of our region, and those of us living in the Pacific Northwest are never far from its waters. It seems appropriate that the research of the river's historical photography should be centered in Wenatchee, a historic gathering place near a midpoint on this great river.

We in Wenatchee spend our lives observing and experiencing the river. The city is located on a wide bend, so each day we look both up and down the river. As we watch the Columbia's flowing waters, we may contemplate its chaotic birth among the tall crags and jagged peaks of verdant Canadian mountains. Strolling our riverfront park trails with a view downstream, we see the Columbia traveling through harshly beautiful shrub-steppe landscapes, past basaltic outcrops, dry coulees, cactus-strewn mesas, and parched desert hillsides sprinkled glorious green by irrigated orchards. We know that these waters will soon enter the scenic Columbia Gorge and, thereafter, cross the Columbia Bar to enter the Pacific.

This book, and the museum exhibition from which it grew, provides a view of the Great River that no one has seen for decades. William Layman has given us all a book of beauty that illustrates humankind's interaction with and dependence upon this incredible everlasting resource, the "being" that is the Columbia River.

The Wenatchee Valley Museum & Cultural Center is grateful to the many institutions, foundations, and individuals who have helped realize the dream to return visual memory to the Columbia River. We hope that the exhibition as well as this book will always lead you back to her waters and that you will celebrate the beauty of life along her shores.

—Dr. Keith Williams, Director
Wenatchee Valley Museum & Cultural Center

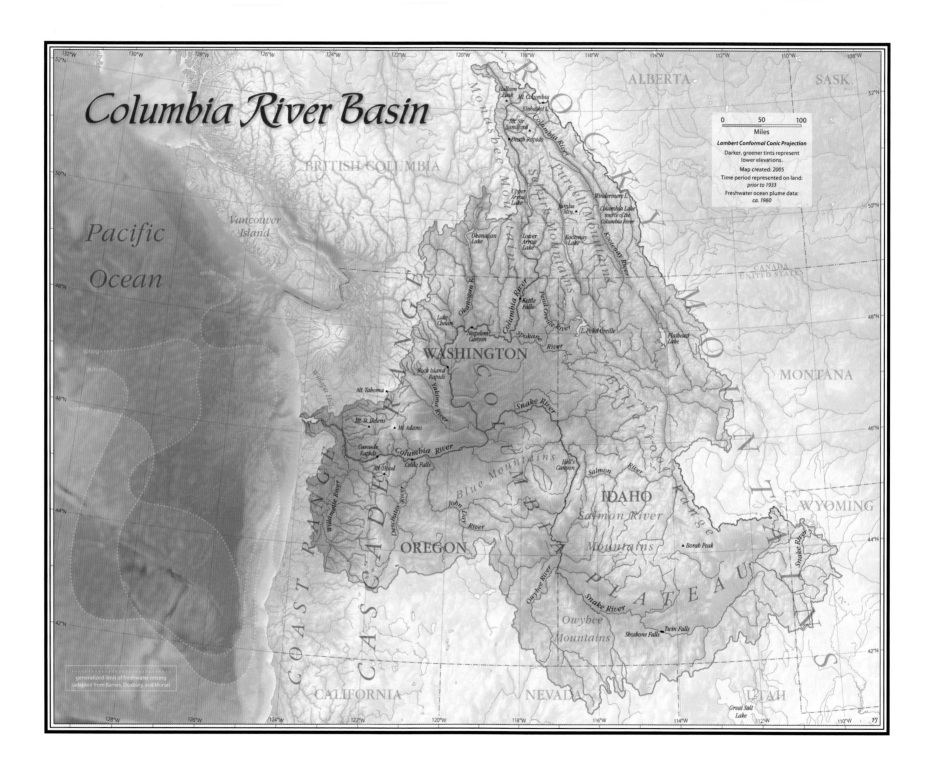

Columbia River Basin

Pacific
Ocean

Vancouver
Island

BRITISH COLUMBIA

ALBERTA

SASK.

0   50   100
Miles

Lambert Conformal Conic Projection

Darker, greener tints represent
lower elevations.

Map created: 2005

Time period represented on land:
prior to 1933

Freshwater ocean plume data:
ca. 1960

ROCKY MOUNTAIN

Hallam Peak
Mt. Columbia
Kinbasket L.
Mt. Sir Sandford
Death Rapids

Columbia River

Upper Arrow Lake

Windermere L.
Jumbo Mtn.
Columbia Lake source of the Columbia River

Okanogan Lake

Lower Arrow Lake

Selkirk Mountains

Purcell Mountains

Kootenay Lake

Kootenay River

Okanogan R.

Columbia River

Kettle Falls

Pend Oreille River

L. Pend Oreille

Flathead Lake

CANADA
UNITED STATES

Lake Chelan

Nespelem Canyon

Spokane River

MONTANA

WASHINGTON

Rock Island Rapids

Yakima River

BITTERROOT RANGE

Mt. Tahoma

COLUMBIA

Snake River

Mt. St. Helens
Mt. Adams

Cascade Rapids
Columbia River
Mt. Hood
Celilo Falls

Blue Mountains

Hell's Canyon

IDAHO

Salmon River

Salmon River Mountains

Borah Peak

WYOMING

John Day River

Deschutes River

Willamette River

CASCADE RANGE

OREGON

COAST RANGE

Owyhee River

Snake River

PLATEAU

Owyhee Mountains

Shoshone Falls
Twin Falls

Snake River

winter

spring

autumn

summer

Willapa Hills

CALIFORNIA

NEVADA

UTAH

Great Salt Lake

generalized limit of freshwater mixing
(adapted from Barnes, Duxbury, and Morse)

PJ

Introduction

The Columbia River begins at the head of a lake in a quiet swamp where reeds take root and the water is pure. Three magnificent mountain ranges in British Columbia—the Purcells, Selkirks, and Canadian Rockies—tower over wetlands that comprise its first 120 miles. Before the river was transformed into a large reservoir behind Mica Dam, mountains forced the young river to narrow, giving rise to a continuous series of rapids approaching Boat Encampment, where the Columbia takes its first and most dramatic bend. Heading south toward Arrow Lakes, the river follows a large valley where a chain of volcanic islands joined the ancient margin of the North American continent 180 million years ago. After entering the United States, the river encounters the great basalt formations of the region's interior that effectively block its southern passage. In a masterful work of yielding, the river skirts these basalts before cutting through them at Rock Island Rapids. A short distance from its confluence with the Snake River, the Columbia turns westward toward the heart of the Cascade Mountains. Threading a path through mountains framed by volcanoes and waterfalls, the big river creates landscapes of grandeur that have inspired all who pass along its shores. After emerging from the gorge, the river's most difficult work is done. Now widened and stately, it flows through the Coastal Range to join the sea in fullness, replenishing the great Pacific with billions of gallons of fresh water per day.

Into all this water come salmon, wave after wave, run after run. Two centuries ago the numbers were astonishing: in a good year, sixteen million of these magnificent fish entered the river, forging ahead with an inner mandate to find the waters where life began. Poet Tim McNulty expresses the relationship well: "The salmon's heart is the river's heart made flesh. Ours is the wisdom to see them both as one."

Between the years 1933 to 1984, public and private utilities along with the governments of the United States and Canada initiated an unparalleled fervor of engineering that transformed much of the Columbia into a series of large reservoirs crossed by fourteen dams. While many grieved the loss of the free-flowing river, the majority of Pacific Northwest citizens embraced a newly tamed river that would control floods, irrigate parched lands, and supply electrical power to match the fast pace of twentieth-century invention and need. Little attention was given to looking back at what was lost. Even the otherwise earth-friendly *National Geographic* published an article in 1942 praising the charming man-made lakes that were superseding "ugly lava chasms" along the river course.

The older, unaltered Columbia shaped the lifeways and character of humans and fish alike. Indigenous people representing four primary language groups developed distinct cultures deeply attuned to the river's life-giving waters and seasonal flows. The river provided nourishment, shelter, and

The Dalles, 2004   Collection of the Author

means of movement to people living along its shores as well as to some forty-six native species of fish living within its waters. Dace, sticklebacks, sculpins, suckers, minnows, eels, and salmon all found special niches in the river, their bodies and behaviors shaped by and attuned to what the river's changing flow offered. Indigenous respect and knowledge extends to other fish besides the all-important salmon—many of these fish figure into the myths and understandings connecting people to place. Suckers prepare the river for the coming of salmon; sculpins have power to predict the weather. In the Ancient Time, Water Monster lurked beneath the river's whirlpools and fast waters, threatening to swallow the Animal People who preceded humans. Water Monster's pet, the white sturgeon, measures up to twenty feet and still swims along the river's bottom.

In a sense, two Columbia Rivers flow through our lives—the river we see today and the natural river that gave rise to the

spectacular sights and thunderings of such places as Celilo and Kettle falls. To know either has always presented major challenges. Certainly this was so for the huge Chinook salmon that swam and leapt more than twelve hundred miles to reach the river's headwaters at Columbia Lake. The same applies to the small number of people who have traversed the length of its waters by bateaux, canoe, or kayak. One person, river advocate Christopher Swain, recently came to know the challenges of the modern Columbia firsthand by swimming its entire length of 1,243 miles, stroke by stroke.

Unlike humans, fish travel easily between the United States and Canada without encountering barriers. The international border at the 49th parallel has effectively established a corresponding internal boundary that limits knowing the river as a whole. While hydroelectric development along the river has brought enormous regional benefits, the creation of the Columbia's massive dams has also obscured aspects of the river's

The Dalles, 1887   Oregon Historical Society, OrHi 11945

identity. When going over the river's bridges, travelers read signs indicating that they are crossing the Columbia, yet people tend to regard the vast reservoir behind Grand Coulee Dam only as Lake Roosevelt, failing to recognize it as the river people once knew. A highway heading north out of Wenatchee has a sign that reads, "Rocky Reach Reservoir, Lake Entiat," making no mention at all of the Columbia.

In truth, the Columbia was never an easy river to know. If the legendary explorer David Thompson were alive today, he would certainly concur—it took him all of four years to track the river to the sea. Some historians fault Thompson for not finding the fabled Northwest Passage sooner, but his confusion remains understandable. Rather than flowing south, the river illogically heads north from its source at Columbia Lake. Confounding the river's geographic puzzle, the Kootenay River, one of the Columbia's primary tributaries, is already a full-fledged stream charging southward within a few miles of the Columbia's

headwaters. Further, the river's rugged physical character prevents knowing by slicing through inaccessible mountain ranges, vast stretches of unpopulated roadless areas, and extreme landscapes before emptying into the sea.

This complexity of the Columbia's natural and cultural worlds provides unending fascination and allure. Author Gretel Ehrlich writes, "To trace the history of a river is to trace the history of the soul." Rivers are an archetypal presence within the human psyche. They orient us to who we are as well as to our place in the world. A river, like a person, carries a singular identity; but, paradoxically, its waters are never quite the same from one moment to the next. Looking upstream we ponder origins; Pacific Northwest residents begin to think forested mountains, snowmelt, and glacial ice. Turning downriver the views change, as do our thoughts. We wonder what lies beyond the next bend. Ultimately, rivers teach us that soon enough we all flow into the limitless wisdom of the ocean.

Imagining these altered landscapes goes beyond a fleeting exercise of the imagination. Ponder the views well and soon you are confronted with what historian William Lang identifies as "important and vexatious questions about the meaning of place" that force us to consider the connections landscapes have with human community. In harnessing the Columbia for our own pleasures, needs, and ends, in what ways have we lost connection to the river's natural world and, in turn, to our interior selves? For those who identify strongly with the Columbia's waters, the remembered river brings a mix of feelings to the surface. Many who view these photographs are likely to experience sadness and grief. Yet the Columbia offers much more; the memory of its noisy waters rushing around rock formations and over Celilo and Kettle falls stimulates wonder and awe, and, for some, a feeling of comfort in knowing that somewhere beneath its present waters the Columbia's spirit remains wild.

The field of Columbia River studies has never been stronger. A generation ago a small bookcase could hold all of the writings that focused solely on the river. Interest picked up sharply with the rise of ecological awareness during the 1970s. A wealth of new publications ably spoke to the river's rich geologic, natural, and cultural histories. Following the completion of Revelstoke Dam in 1984, collective attention in both the United States and Canada shifted from impounding more water to enhancing the river's capacity to sustain biologic health while allowing for human use. Our society is learning that, ultimately, the Columbia's sustainability is critical to our own. First Nations tribes of Canada, American Indian tribes of the United States, environmental and consumer groups, educational institutions, the hydroelectric industry, and government agencies alike are working to address the difficult issues involved in creating a healthy balance for the river and its inhabitants. These dynamics and more will be examined fully as the United States

and Canada set about the task of renewing the Columbia River Treaty, a process that is likely to begin formally in 2014.

Geologists tell us that the Columbia has been around for some five million years and there is no end in sight. With this in mind, the Wenatchee Valley Museum & Cultural Center has named the exhibition *River of Memory: The Everlasting Columbia*. Gathering the project's materials has been like restringing a beautiful necklace whose beads became separated from the original strand. Over time, images documenting the river have found their way into the recesses of private collections, libraries, museums, and archives throughout the United States and Canada. We were especially interested in locating those views that depict less well-known river places. Other sections of river presented the opposite problem. Within the eighty-mile stretch of Columbia Gorge, eminent photographers of the nineteenth and twentieth centuries visited the gorge to record its scenic wonders on glass plates and film. Up until the last salmon arrived at Celilo Falls, countless individuals trained their lenses to document the extraordinary scene of Indians extending dip nets into the swirling waters below the falls. The Celilo photographs speak through the ages; when they are placed alongside those taken up and down the river, a picture of the whole river begins to emerge, connecting tributaries, mountains, and histories to water, earth, and sky.

From the exhibit's inception we wished to include the river's aquatic residents who have known the Columbia intimately for eons. Joseph Tomelleri's and Dan McConnell's exquisite illustrations of fish became the basis for the creation of silk paintings produced for the exhibit. In addition, we sought the strong voices of American and Canadian poets and writers whose words could help us linger along the river's native shorelines.

River travelers know it is easier to move with the river's current than against it. We preferred the more strenuous upriver

Lake Windermere

Ryan Bavin, November 2002   Wenatchee Valley Museum & Cultural Center, 005-53-5

journey in homage to salmon and other fish returning to natal waters from the sea. This corresponds to the indigenous belief that the salmon are ancestors who have made the arduous journey of return for the benefit of all.

The Wenatchee Valley Museum & Cultural Center created *River of Memory: The Everlasting Columbia* to bring the images of the natural river into collective awareness. Elders within the region still remember the river's great expanse and fast waters, but with each passing year fewer remain. In the not-too-distant future the last person holding living memory of Celilo and

Kettle falls will have died. For some, the old river is like a special grandparent who passed away before we were born. We grew up hearing his or her stories, and something within us longs to be in this special person's presence, even if just for a moment. Our museum believes that people living here a thousand years from now will carry the same yearning to know the grandfather-grandmother-father-mother river. May these views, illustrations, narratives, and poems foster a new intimacy and connection that brings people into an ever-deepening relationship to this special Northwest place—the Great River of the West.

—William D. Layman, April 2006

River of Memory

The Everlasting Columbia

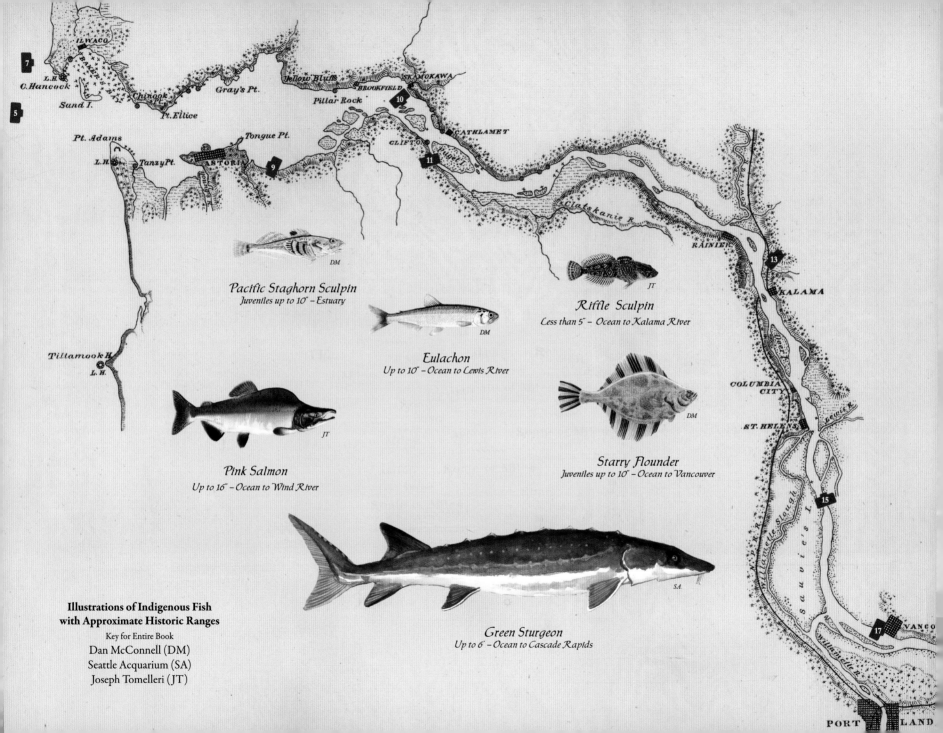

Pacific Staghorn Sculpin
Juveniles up to 10" – Estuary

Eulachon
Up to 10" – Ocean to Lewis River

Riffle Sculpin
Less than 5" – Ocean to Kalama River

Pink Salmon
Up to 16" – Ocean to Wind River

Starry Flounder
Juveniles up to 10" – Ocean to Vancouver

Green Sturgeon
Up to 6' – Ocean to Cascade Rapids

**Illustrations of Indigenous Fish
with Approximate Historic Ranges**
Key for Entire Book
Dan McConnell (DM)
Seattle Acquarium (SA)
Joseph Tomelleri (JT)

The Mouth of the Columbia to Celilo Falls

River Miles 1 to 200.5

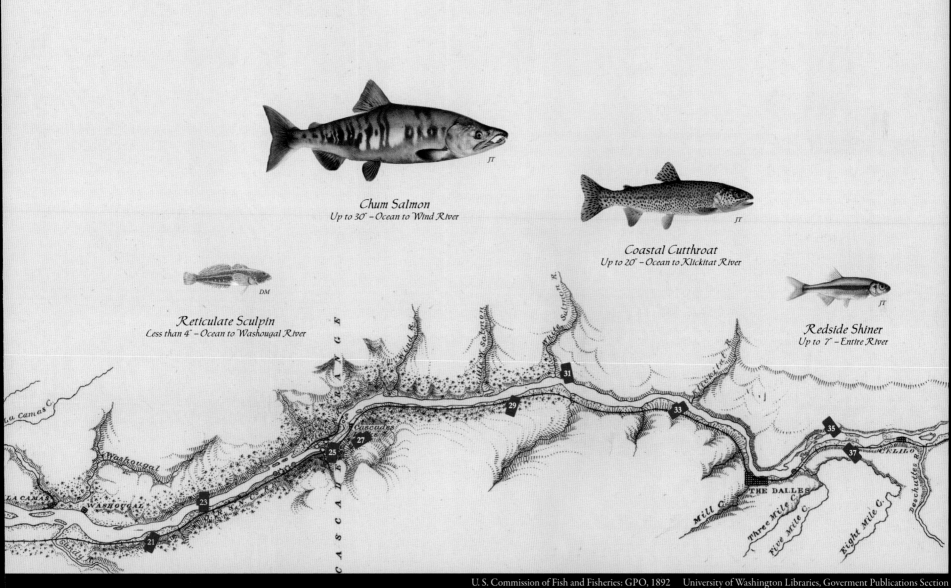

Chum Salmon
Up to 30" – Ocean to Wind River

Coastal Cutthroat
Up to 20" – Ocean to Klickitat River

Reticulate Sculpin
Less than 4" – Ocean to Washougal River

Redside Shiner
Up to 7" – Entire River

So strong is this river that its flume in spring extends
hundreds of miles out to sea. Salmon traveling the sweep
of Pacific Rim currents sense the Columbia's freshwater
traces and immediately turn to follow its distinctive
signature. Thousands upon thousands gather in pools just
beyond the sandbars. Ranging in size from one pound
to seventy and in age from two years to seven, their sleek
bodies adjust as they wait for tides to carry them over the
treacherous sandbars to the calmer waters of the estuary.
Moving with floodtides and ebbs, the fish make headway,
fall back, and swim forward again. Initially it takes a day to
gain each mile upriver. By the time the runs pass Bradley
Point, forty-four miles inland, the salmon are traveling six
to ten miles per day on their upriver quest of return.

Chinook Salmon (ocean phase)
Up to 60″ – Ocean to Source (before obstructions)

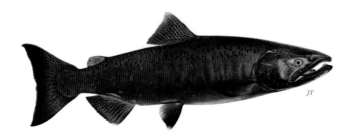

Chinook Salmon (spawning male)
Up to 60″ – Ocean to Source (before obstructions)

Mouth of Columbia River from the Pacific Ocean
Brubaker Aerial Survey, 1929   NARA Pacific Alaska Region (Seattle), RG77, Portland District, L-224

1,243 miles to source

Colliding forces of strong winds pushing the sea shoreward
and outgoing tides from the swollen river occasionally
create spectacular waves along the shallow sandbars
stretched across the river's mouth. Prior to the large dams
that now regulate the flow of spring freshets, old-timers
reported seeing hundred-foot waves breaking along the
sandbar's shallow waters, challenging all who would pass
into the river. Over the years the entrance to the river
has acquired the name "Graveyard of the Pacific," having
claimed over two thousand ships and more than fifteen
hundred lives where its turbulent waters meet the sea.

Cape Disappointment

Josef Scaylea, ca.1955   Wenatchee Valley Museum & Cultural Center, 005-53-1

At the river's mouth
1,243 miles to source

The river expands to nearly nine miles in width just beyond Astoria. Here, a peninsula—aptly named Tongue Point by early explorers—extends several miles into rich estuarine waters. Captain William Clark noted that the water on the upriver side was fresh and fine, while below its taste was salty. Travelers rounding the point frequently encountered strong winds, tides, and currents, necessitating unanticipated layovers and miserably wet portages. Numerous Cathlamet and Chinook native villages once nestled along the river among stands of cedar and spruce, trees that provided raw materials for baskets, shelters, clothing, and the magnificent canoes that could once be seen moving up and down the lower river. The Columbia today retains a rugged beauty. Just beyond Tongue Point, the Lewis and Clark Wildlife Refuge protects the many birds, mammals, and fish that live in and around the lower Columbia's waters.

There are those to whom place is unimportant,
But this place, where sea and fresh water meet,
Is important—
Where the hawks sway out into the wind,
Without a single wingbeat,
And the eagles sail low over the fir trees,
And the gulls cry against the crows
in the curved harbors,
And the tide rises up against the grass
nibbled by sheep and rabbits.

—Theodore Roethke
from "The Rose"

Tongue Point Looking Downriver

Brubaker Aerial Survey, May 6, 1929   NARA Pacific Alaska Region (Seattle), RG77, Portland District

18 miles from ocean
1,125 miles to source

Tenasillahe Island
Brubaker Aerial Survey, ca. 1930
NARA Pacific Alaska Region (Seattle), RG77, Portland District

Smooth waters
conceal swirling energies

islands wrapped in clouds
hold ancestral memory

—William Layman

Waters issuing from innumerable rivulets, thousands of streams, and a hundred rivers continually bring minerals and sediments downstream where they settle in the riverbed. Heavier boulders and rocks remain close to their place of origin, blocking the river's flow while at the same time providing habitat for fish. Gravel and sand particles travel greater distances, especially during the spring freshets. The finer silts build up over time to form the numerous islands in the lower stretches of river, while other sediments travel out to sea to form sandbars at the river's mouth or great sand beaches stretching for miles up and down the coastline.

35 miles from ocean
1,208 miles to source

COLUMBIA RIVER FROM BRADLEY PARK · 728 EDDY

Puget Island

Ralph Eddy RPPC, ca. 1915   Steven Lehl Collection

44 miles from ocean
1,199 miles to source

Kelso Road down the Columbia River

A.N. Bush, July 20, 1915   Bush House Museum, bhp 0039

71 miles from ocean
1,172 miles to source

In winter and early spring the Columbia's shorelines above the Lewis River harbor the same wild sounds of migratory birds that caused William Clark to go sleepless on the night of March 29, 1805. Throughout the summer and fall months, the mosaic of riverine floodplain on Sauvie Island nourished the Multnomah Indians with the highly valued wappato, a wild potato that Native women harvested by lifting the roots from the river bottom with curled toes while standing waist-deep in water. Even before the first visit by Euroamericans, smallpox and other diseases had decimated the people, painfully preparing the way for the rush of settlement that by 1857 was in full swing. Today, along protected tracts of wetlands bordering both sides of the river, large concentrations of geese and swans rise in the air with the same strength and voice they have known for millennia.

Lower Sauvie Island Facing Downriver

Brubaker Aerial Survey, January 4, 1934   NARA Pacific Alaska Region (Seattle), RG77, Portland District, L-276

88 miles from ocean
1,155 miles to source

The volcanoes in our stories moved and lived before
our human presence. They made way for the contour of
skyline. The river shifted this way, left its mark. It made
a way for us. Coyote walked here and made this so in this
time's beginning. Songs are sung through our lives and
are a part of how we follow. There is a difference here.
We dream. We know our bodies are made of all these
elements. On this land we are all motion. We age.
Society changes. New people arrive. Old people
leave. Memory stays.

—Elizabeth Woody
from "Recognition of the Maker"

COPYRIGHT,
KISER PHOTOGRAPHIC CO.

MT. HOOD AND COLUMBIA RIVER, FROM VANCOUVER, WASH.

Mount Hood from Vancouver
Fred and Oscar Kiser, ca. 1910   John McClelland Jr. Collection

Mountains rising four thousand feet above the always changing river, waterfalls issuing from green canyon walls, pinnacles punctuating landscapes, and promontories jutting from the river's edge combine to give the Columbia Gorge its extraordinary nature. From the lush forests of Crown Point to the barren basalt exposures beyond The Dalles, the Columbia offers one spectacular view after another—it is as though the river course connects two entirely different worlds.

Annual rainfall diminishes from one hundred inches at Wind River to less than fourteen inches at The Dalles. The Columbia Gorge becomes in effect a barometric equalizer, mediating weather from each side of the Cascade Range to produce the legendary air currents that early boaters feared.

Rich in human history, Cascade Rapids, The Narrows, and Celilo Falls were once among the world's most productive fisheries. Though these places are now flooded, Native American elders and families gather at Celilo each spring to pray, feast, and acknowledge the salmon's yearly return.

The Columbia is everywhere beautiful, but here in the Gorge it rises to heights of sublimity.

—Earl Roberge

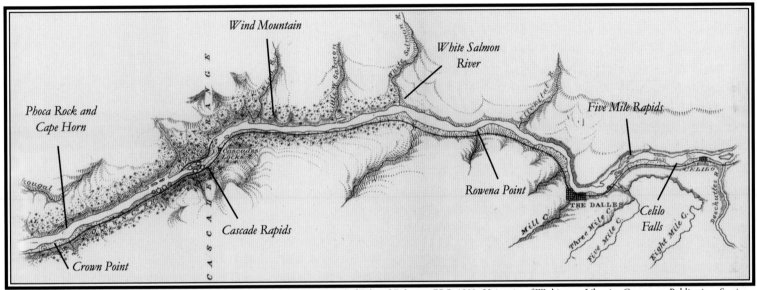

US Commission of Fish and Fisheries: GPO, 1892. University of Washington Libraries, Goverment Publications Section

Leopard Dace
*Up to 4" – From Cowlitz River
to Lower Arrow Lakes*

Speckled Dace
Up to 4" – Up to Pend O'reilleRiver

Umatilla Dace
*Up to 4" – From Umatilla River
to outlet of Lower Arrow Lakes*

Congnose Dace
Up to 4" – Entire River

The Columbia's great might derives from its steep descent out of the mountains of Canada. Between Crown Point and its source at Columbia Lake, the river drops an average of twenty-seven inches per mile. After cutting through the Columbia Gorge, the river's downward thrust eases, dropping less than four inches per mile until it meets the ocean. Even this far upstream, the last vestiges of tidal influence create a gentle rise and fall along the shorelines of Reed and Sand islands to the east of Crown Point.

Ancient inland seas, massive volcanic flows, warpings of the earth's crust, and the largest floods in history reveal a complex story of the Columbia's persistence in finding new ways to reach the sea. East of Crown Point conglomerates from the Troutdale Formation reveal that the modern river was preceded by one of the two ancestral rivers that flowed south of the present-day course. Two-hundred-million-year-old pebbles of quartzite with origins in the mountains of Canada traveled over a thousand miles of ancestral river to reach an eventual placement by the river's edge. The first of these ancestral rivers joined the modern river channel at Crown Point.

Sunset on the Columbia

Cross and Dimmitt RPPC, ca. 1915   Wenatchee Valley Museum & Cultural Center, 005-53-3

116 miles from ocean
1,127 miles to source

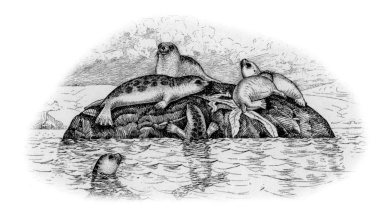

U. S. Report of the Commissioner of Fish and Fisheries, 1880
Collection of the Author

On their seaward journey, Lewis and Clark saw dark
heads of mammals they identified as sea otters swimming
through the waters of Columbia Gorge. Later when
wintering at Fort Clatsop, they learned they were
mistaken; what they had seen were harbor seals hunting
the fall run of salmon. Perhaps members of the expedition
observed several resting on this solitary islet that stands in
the middle of the river just past Cape Horn. Clark named
the island Phoca Rock on his map. Increasing numbers of
seals and sea lions in recent years have followed salmon
to the base of Bonneville Dam below the former Cascade
Rapids where each animal consumes up to ten fish per day.

Phoca Rock

D. C. Herrin, 1894   Steven Lehl Collection

133 miles from ocean
1,110 miles to source

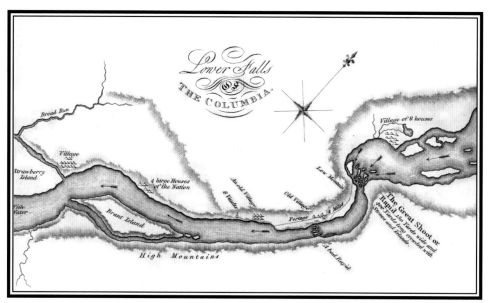

Lower Falls of the Columbia, 1814
Manuscripts, Archives and Special Collections, Washington State University Libraries, wsu 557

*This Great Shute or falls is about 1/2 a mile, with the water
of this great river compressed within the space of 150 paces in
which there is great numbers of both large and Small rocks,
water passing with great velocity, forming [foaming]
& boiling in a most horriable manner, with a fall of about
20 feet, below it wides to about 200 paces and current gentle
for a Short Distance.*

—Captain William Clark, Oct. 31, 1805
Journals of Lewis and Clark

Lower Cascade Rapids Looking Downstream

Copied by Asahel Curtis from Thompsen, ca. 1897   Washington State Historical Society, 34048

147 miles from ocean
1,096 miles to source

Cascade Rapids with Fisherman

A man stands by the river.
All-that-was flows away.

A woman sits by the river.
All-that-will-be is coming.

A child, in shredded cedarbark, gazes.
At the portage, the people are traveling.

The elders have learned to be still.
The river is teaching, remembering prophecy:

Salmon goes upriver.
The fine bones tumble down.

Is the wind a different fluency than water?
Is a child's long cry a river disguised?

The river, going down, turns over.
All flows toward another place.

Those who are gone stand here:
I will await you in the children.

—Kim Stafford

Upper Cascade Rapids
Carleton E. Watkins, 1882–1883   Steven Lehl Collection

Wind Mountain from Mitchell Point

Joseph Gallio Masters, ca. 1915–35   Denver Public Library, Z-6562

161 miles from ocean
1,082 miles to source

Legendary winds and waves of the Columbia Gorge provide modern-day river users sun-filled days of gusty pleasure. Not so for early river travelers such as the Reverend Jason Lee whose missionary zeal led him to enlist the help of four Indians to ferry him upriver in the winter of 1843.

Wednesday, January 31. Snow fell several inches during the night and continued to fall in the morning. Breakfast and prayers over, we transferred our luggage to the canoe and set forward. . . . Our breeze soon increased to a gale, which rendered our condition perilous. The river soon became dreadfully agitated, and our situation became more and more dangerous. The wind was on our quarter, and, with our blanket-sail, which we had rigged early in the day, we were able to drive before the waves except when we were retarded by the islands of floating snow and ice. To land was impossible. By laying as closely to the wind as possible we could just clear the rugged points of ice which had formed out from the shore and the rocky bluffs which rose in awful sublimity over our heads. . . . The waves began to break over our boat and the man at the stern sang out lustily, "Pull away!" as our only hope of safety. We saw a mountain wave coming, but could not escape it entirely. It broke over our quarter and nearly engulfed the man at the helm, and left a great quantity of water thick with snow and ice in our canoe. Fortunately we were soon through the snow, and were able to clear a point of rocks which we were in imminent danger of being dashed upon.

—H. K. Hines, D. D.
Missionary History of the Pacific Northwest, 1899

Cascade Mountain Range near White Salmon

Lily White or Sarah H. Ladd, 1902–1903   Oregon Historical Society, OrHi 65456

170 miles from ocean
1,073 miles to source

*Upon learning of the Gorge's dramatic landscapes, well
known photographers of the nineteenth century boarded
steamers and trains to experience and record its wonders.
Carleton Watkins, already highly regarded for his stunning
mammoth albumen photographic prints taken of the
Columbia River in 1867, visited the river again between
1882 and 1884, this time turning his lens toward less obvious
views that show the nuances and beauty of shoreline sites. In
this photograph Watkins has purposefully embraced the hazy
and diffuse light of an autumn afternoon in the eastern Gorge.
Looking across the river, we are made aware of his deliberate
emphasis on atmospheric haze as a visible and integral
quality of the season. As if to further clarify his intent, the
photographer has included a substantial portion of shoreline
in the foreground, rendered in rich and contrasting tones.*

—Terry Toedtemeier

Indian Summer on the Columbia

Carleton E. Watkins, 1882–1883   Phoebe Apperson Hearst Museum of Anthropology, 13-1302x

179 miles from ocean
1,064 miles to source

The narrowing of the river at Three-Mile, Five-Mile, and Ten-Mile rapids within The Dalles offered ideal fishing for Wishram Indians living on the north bank and Wasco Indians occupying the south bank. Through long winter nights people waited for the season's turning. After the first roots appeared in spring, villagers watched the river intently, eager for the salmon's return. The first salmon brought from the river was a high point of the year, a cause for joy and celebration accompanied by prayer, dancing, and feasting. After ceremonies, the first salmon's bones were reverently returned to the river.

Five-Mile Rapids
Lily White, 1902–1903   Private Collection

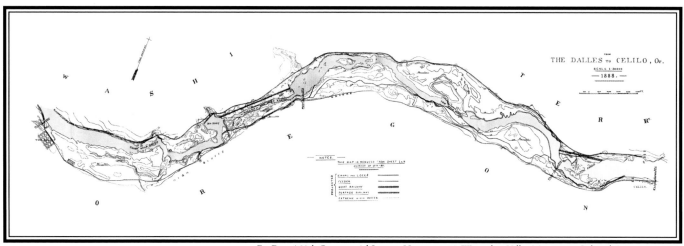

Ex. Doc. / 50th Congress, 2d Session, House; no. 73, Wenatchee Valley Museum & Cultural Center, 005-53-7

The Dalles

Albert H. Wulzen, 1887   Oregon Historical Society, OrHi 11945

At the Dalles the vast river is jammed together into a long, narrow slot of unknown depth cut sheer down in the basalt. This slot or trough is about a mile and a half long and about sixty yards wide at the narrowest place. At ordinary times the river seems to be set on edge and runs swiftly but without much noisy surging with a descent of about twenty feet to the mile. But when the snow is melting on the mountains the river rises here sixty feet, or even more during extraordinary freshets, and spreads out over a great breadth of massive rocks through which have been cut several other gorges running parallel with the one usually occupied. All these inferior gorges now come into use, and the huge, roaring torrent,

still rising and spreading, at length overwhelms the high jagged rock walls between them, making a tremendous display of chafing, surging, shattered currents, counter-currents, and hollow whirls that no words can be made to describe. A few miles between the Dalles the storm-tossed river gets itself together again, looks like water, becomes silent and with stately, tranquil deliberation goes on its way, out of the gray region of sage and sand into the Oregon woods.

—John Muir
Picturesque California and the Region
West of the Rocky Mountains, from Alaska to Mexico

196 miles from ocean
1,047 miles to source

*Celilo Falls is a jumble of huge rock piles and sheer drops
over which the untamed Columbia hurls itself in thundering
abandon. Below the falls, boiling whirlpools hiss and roar,
whipping and splashing high into the air. . . . Thousands
of silver fish fling themselves against the tumbling cascades
of rushing water whose roar and the violent motion of the
salmon, fill one's senses. . . . Rickety platforms hang in midair
above the turbulent water, flimsy structures of wood attached
to the rocks in seemingly makeshift fashion. On these frail-
looking perches, men of the tribes take turns fishing. Each uses
a net with a 20-foot handle, thrusting it upstream as far as
he can reach and allowing the current to carry it downstream
with its open end facing the fish that are swimming up.
Salmon are so plentiful that there's not a break in the action,
but a constant rhythm of thrust, drift, and capture. Each
netted fish is herded toward the riverbank, where another
fisherman removes it, clubs it, and tosses it into a large basket,
then turns to wrestle with the next one.*

—Dorothea Nordstrand
"The Celilo Falls That Used to Be"
Columbia Magazine, Fall 2001

Celilo Falls

Amos Burg, ca. 1926   Oregon Historical Society, OrHi 105335

200.5 miles from ocean
1,042.5 miles to source

Celilo (Wyam) Root Feast and Salmon 2005

Loss of Wyam caused pervasive sadness, even in celebratory events. The old Longhouse is gone. The Wyam, or Celilo Falls, are gone. Still courage, wisdom, strength and belief bring us together each season to speak to all directions the ancient words. There is no physical Celilo, but we have our mothers, fathers, sisters, brothers, and our children bound together for all possible life in the future. We are salmon (Waykanash). We are deer (Winat). We are roots (Xnit). We are berries (Tmanit). We are water (Chuush). We are the animation of the Creator's wisdom in Worship song (Waashat Walptaikash).

The spirit of the "Place of Echoing Water upon Rocks" is not silent. We care for the river and the life of traditional unity, the humble dignity, and purity in intention— wholeness. Ultimately, we restore life with our attention and devotion. Each hears the echoing water within.

The leader speaks in the ancient language's manner. He speaks to all in Ichiskiin. He says, "We are following our ancestors. We respect the same Creator and the same religion, each in turn of their generation, and conduct the same service and dance to honor our relatives, the roots, and the salmon. The Creator at the beginning of time gave us instruction and the wisdom to live the best life. The Creator made man and woman with independent minds. We must choose to live by the law, as all the others, salmon, trees, water, air, all live by it. We must use all the power of our minds and hearts to bring the salmon back. Our earth needs our commitment. That is our teachings. We are each powerful and necessary."

All lift their hands palms open and upward to acknowledge and recognize the speaker's truth: the presence of the Creator's strength is among us and inside us. The words enter the greater and expansive essence of living earth. We are land. We are water. Our passion is the fire in our home's hearth. We all exchange the same air in exclamation. We are all one.

—Elizabeth Woody
Spellings courtesy of Arlita Rhoan and Dallas Winishut
Confederated Tribes of Warm Springs, Oregon

Celilo Falls at High Water

D. C. Herrin, April 24, 1894   Collection of the Author

200.5 miles from ocean
1,042.5 miles to source

Celilo Falls to Snake River

River Miles 200.5 to 324

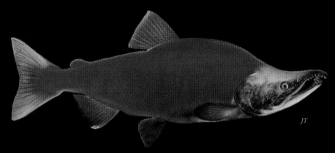

Sockeye Salmon (male)
Up to 30" – Ocean to Inlet of Upper Arrow Lake (before obstructions)

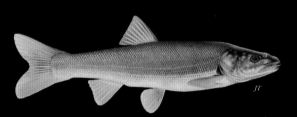

Northern Pikeminnow
Up to 24" – Entire River

Redband Trout
Up to 24" – Entire River

Mountain Sucker
Up to 9" – From Cowlitz River to Wenatchee River

White Sturgeon
Up to 20' – Ocean to Kinbasket Lake (before obstructions)

WAR DEPT.
OFFICE EXPLORATIONS AND SURVEYS

MAP OF
MILITARY RECONNAISSANCE
FROM
FORT DALLES, OREGON, VIA FORT WALLAH-WALLAH,
TO
FORT TAYLOR, WASHINGTON TERRITORY,

made under direction of CAPT. A. A. HUMPHREYS, U.S. Top.¹ Eng.ʳˢ,

by Lieut. JOHN MULLAN, U.S. Army,

assisted by

THEODORE KOLECKI and GUSTAVUS SOHON, Civil Eng.ʳˢ,

while attached to the Military Expedition under

COL. GEO. WRIGHT, 9.ᵗʰ Infantry, in

1858.

Scale... 1:300,000.

Explanation.

Note. The ravens indicate not an elevation of 200 feet (continental). The only exception being those in Wallah Wallah Valley, showing the small dividing ridges between the numerous little streams, which are only from 15 to 30 feet high.

Paiute Sculpin

Columbia Sculpin (Mottled Sculpin)
Up to 5" – From Cowlitz River to outlet of Lower Arrow Lake

By carefully placing rocks in the river, indigenous people created eddies and chutes that facilitated fishing. But when need called for sternwheelers moving large quantities of grain downriver, nothing short of "river improvement work" was required. Beginning in 1867, army engineers identified problematic stretches of water and gave men diamond bits and drills along with large quantities of blasting dynamite to clear the obstructions. The first such project along the Columbia targeted John Day's Rock at the base of the rapids, named for a hapless member of John Jacob Astor's expedition. Working in isolation and under extreme winter weather conditions, crews drilled numerous holes into the hard basalt and set off explosion after explosion. Within ten years, engineers had removed troublesome rocks and ledges at Squally Hook, Rock Creek, Owyhee and Umatilla Rapids. The work was always dangerous; in 1876 a premature detonation killed thirteen men at Umatilla Rapids.

When the current pours over a sunken rock having three or four feet on it, the water forms large waves, extending from 50 to 200 feet on the down-stream side of the rock. Some of the waves are very large. . . . Another great difficulty in making the survey was owing to the presence of whirls in the river. On many of the rapids where large rocks were exposed, the current would be divided by these rocks and these divisions would again come in contact on the lower side of the rocks which would cause immense whirls, some of them 12 feet in diameter by 5 feet deep in the center, being very much like an inverted cone. They would gradually work down the river until they became smaller and smaller, and would finally disappear.

Annual Report of the Chief of Engineers 1868

John Day Rapids

Asahel Curtis, April 1, 1929   Washington State Historical Society, 54790

218 miles from ocean
1,025 miles to source

Ask Me

Some time when the river is ice ask me
mistakes I have made. Ask me whether
what I have done is my life. Others
have come in their slow way into
my thought, and some have tried to help
or to hurt: ask me what difference
their strongest love or hate has made.

I will listen to what you say.
You and I can turn and look
at the silent river and wait. We know
the current is there, hidden; and there
are comings and goings from miles away
that hold the stillness exactly before us.
What the river says, that is what I say.

—William Stafford

Near Rock Creek

United States Army Corps of Engineers, Februrary 22, 1936   NARA Pacific Alaska Region (Seattle), RG77, Portland District (retouched)

Our native land was shaped by the Creator,
    as were we ourselves, with his all-knowing hand.
He put us down amidst these mountains,
    streams, and plains.
Generations of ancestors, unnumbered,
    are buried here beneath this ground.
So surely there can be no wonder
that this land of ours is sacred,
to be protected, and handed on
to generations yet unborn.

                    —Yakama Nation Museum

Blalock Rapids
Asahel Curtis, April 1, 1929   Washington State Historical Society, 54969

236 miles from ocean
1,007 miles to source

Blalock Island

Brubaker Aerial Survey, August 27, 1929   NARA Pacific Alaska Region (Seattle), RG77, Portland District, L-121

276 miles from ocean
967 miles to source

The view looks slightly downriver, accentuating the Columbia's strong lines near its confluence with the Umatilla River. The photographer, Major Lee Moorhouse, has deliberately set his camera back from the rocky shoreline, giving land, river, and sky equal attention. Rounded rocks, cobbles, and boulders in the foreground stand out against the glassy smooth river and cloudless sky. The basalt cliffs, so characteristic of landscapes both up and down the river, are gone; the opposite shore is a treeless straight line rising above the water.

Were it not for the dugout canoe and its two Umatilla occupants, the photograph might hold little interest. Hewn from a single ponderosa pine, the twenty-five-foot vessel faces downstream following the photograph's overall perspective. Yet all is still—still enough for the Umatilla tribesman to confidently stand in the front of his boat. Everything about him speaks of dignity and belonging. Wearing a broad-rimmed hat, a kerchief tied loosely around his neck, and a Pendleton trade blanket tucked around his waist, he looks directly at the photographer. The woman, wearing a Pendleton of more subdued design around her shoulders, holds her paddle so still that it loses itself in the reflected waters. Taken as a whole, the photograph brings together simplicity of form and the solidness of presence, creating a timeless statement about the relationship between people and place.

Near Umatilla Rapids

Major Lee Moorhouse, 1900   Special Collections and University Archives, University of Oregon Libraries, PHO35 6174b

288 miles from ocean
955 miles to source

Wallula Gateway

When cracked earth opened,
fountains of lava spread
across this land

and the ancestral river found
passage through rock
formed by an uplifted ridge.

Ice blocked the river
and vast glacial lakes failed.
Pressures and melt let

wild waters out in a sudden roar.
Here at Wallula, the rising flood climbed
a thousand feet. Rocks and cliffs

broke free, found new places among
downriver sands. Two columns,
after the last flood, remained.

Steadfast sisters gaze at cliffs,
remembering when dark waters
surrounded them in terror.

—William Layman

Wallula Gateway

Snake River to
the International Boundary

River Mile 324 to 725

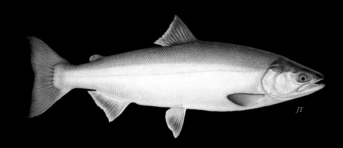

Sockeye Salmon (female)
Up to 30" – Ocean to inlet of Upper Arrow Lake (before obstructions)

Coho Salmon
Up to 38" – Ocean to Kettle Falls

Chiselmouth
Up to 12" – From Cowlitz River to Pend O'reille River

Westslope Cutthroat
Up to 20" – Yakima River to Windermere Lake

Pacific Lamprey
Up to 30" – Ocean to beyond Kootenay River (before obstructions)

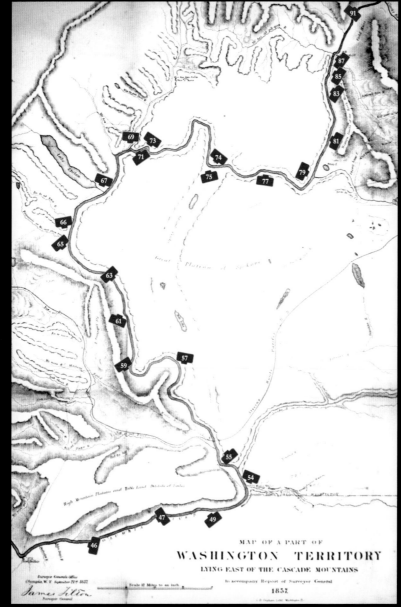

MAP OF A PART OF
WASHINGTON TERRITORY
LYING EAST OF THE CASCADE MOUNTAINS

To accompany Report of Surveyor General
1857

Wenatchee Valley Museum & Cultural Center, 005-53-6

Sandroller
Less than 5" – Estuary to Crescent Bar

Three-Spine Stickleback
*Less than 3" – Ocean and
from Cowlitz River to Methow River*

River Lamprey
Up to 12" – Ocean to White Bluffs

Western Brook Lamprey
Up to 6" – Ocean to Yakima River

The Visible World

From the shore I see the fisherman steer
his small boat through this slow river, past
juts of basalt, greasewood in bloom,
arrowleaf balsam root, and sagebrush, of course.
Further downriver, hugging the cliffs, lies
a section of roadway now going nowhere,
abandoned and broken by rock rose, mullein,
a stand of young birches.

Let us tally the past decades: Subtract a town
that once thrived on the wild river. Deep below
today's quiet surface, an iron ring still digs
into the cliff, a ring paddleboats used to winch
themselves beyond the rapids. Subtract
the sandbars and riverine gullies, petroglyphs
and arrow points, wagons loaded with wheat.
Let the fisherman keep gliding his boat
through the new warmth of this May
morning, let him look down and he will see

Near Mouth of the Walla Walla River
Unknown photographer, undated   Northwest Room, Spokane Public Library

the shadow of a main street, schoolrooms full
of lazy fish, workers' shacks pressed down
by water, silt curling from the chimney
of a chuck house.

Now, in the opening of another summer, the man
and boat create a spun cohesion. He drifts generations
together, and if he kept floating into evening,
he'd witness the depths of privacy, the river sealed up
darkly as if no confluence, no fort and no foot path
ever existed under the heavy ceiling of night.

—Linda Andrews

314 miles from ocean
929 miles to source

COLUMBIA RIVER FROM PASCO·KENNEWICK BRIDGE

Ellis
2866

Columbia River from Pasco-Kennewick Bridge

A reach is our fullest expansion, a dream, a goal, and a stretch toward our maximum potential. A reach is also that gesture of the human arm and soul we use to lean out toward one another. Over chasms of misunderstanding, even war, we reach out to comfort, to support, to understand, and eventually to love. In geography a reach runs between two natural boundaries, usually between two bends. Hanford Reach, one of the Columbia's last expanses of free-flowing river, makes a sharp bend east at Priest Rapids, flows past White Bluffs, a lofty white cliff containing fossils of prehistoric camels, rhinoceros, and mastodon.

—Susan Zwinger

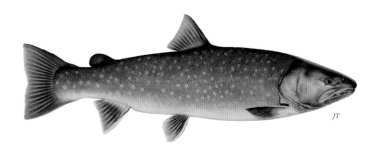

Bull Trout
Up to 36" – Entire River

56

White Bluffs along Hanford Reach

Asahel Curtis, July 9, 1929   Washington State Historical Society, 43022

369 miles from ocean
874 miles to source

I asked Virginia Wyena, an elder at Priest Rapids, about the Indian word for the Columbia, which I understood to be Che Wana, for "big river." I'd seen it written like that or as Chiawana, with four syllables. Just upstream from Priest Rapids I'd passed a railroad siding called Schawana. Was that the same word?

"See? That's just it. Somebody writes it and then people say it wrong. The word is, N'chiawana" and it rolled from her soul off her tongue to fill the world. And for that brief moment I was everywhere on it, like the first time you ever put your ear to a seashell. The word had four syllables, like Chiawana, but it started with an n.

Nchi-a-wah-na, maybe. I asked her to say it again, and she did."N'chiawana"

I tried to say the word. I couldn't say it, not the way she did.

Like you see a white stone in clear deep water, but the act of reaching for it disturbs the water. Then you can't see the stone anymore. You can't find it down there.

I asked her, "How do you spell that?"

"We don't," she said.

—Robin Cody

Priest Rapids

Grace Christiansen Gardner, ca. 1938   Wenatchee Valley Museum & Cultural Center, 40-67-15

397 miles from ocean
846 miles to source

As a Species Flies
From Extinction, Consider
The River

In passing translucence, curled
Feather and flash, see
The brown eyes
Of the world. What rocks
Are these? Fourteen million
Orbits refract this
Onwardness of spreading center, polarity
Spinning a water strider's legs like needles
To the pulse in every
Tongue. Between Kittitas and Whiskey Dick, note
The shape of a bird's sleeping neck
Keeping current through past, holding
The moment ice let go
Mad gleaming, rivulet violence
Starting this etch of avian glyph, this
Fluxing flurry
Bearing the conception:
ending
Is myth, is the syllabics of scree
Clattering before a buck's long skid
And purling swim where the river
He shakes from his antlers,

The river of dazzling droplets,
Freezes the light,
Is the light.

—Derek Sheffield

Above Skookumchuck Creek

Unknown photographer, undated. Grant County Public Utility District

Rock Island Rapids

In the first pages of last century
a person at Rock Island Rapids
could spend a lifetime
and not hear all the notes that played.

Beyond the island's tip
currents race over shallow waters,
yesterday's rain from the mountains
brings new rhythms to shore.

Riffles lap against rocks,
mid-river rapids cascade into each ear—
everywhere a low rumble.

Sounds within sounds,
move two feet or two seconds away,
something entirely new—listen

   it never stops.

                    —William Layman

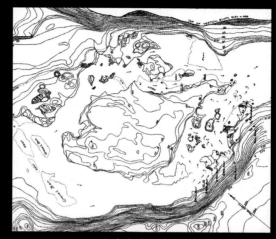

Rock Island Rapids, 1885   WVMCC, 005-53-8

Simmer

Rock Island Rapids, Columbia River. 65

Rock Island Rapids

Harold Simmer, ca. 1925   William Teakle Collection, Northwest Room, Spokane Public Library

By skirting a westerly direction around the immense basalt fields of the Columbia Plateau, the river addresses one problem while moving steadily toward another—the barrier of the Cascade Range. At Wenatchee Flats, the river has pressed westward all it can; it turns south to carve its way through the basalt between Mission Ridge and Badger Mountain at Rock Island Rapids. As with the obstruction at Wallula Gap, early catastrophic flooding created a bottleneck at Rock Island Rapids, temporarily establishing a large lake whose elevation rose to fifteen hundred feet. This backed the river up well beyond Grand Coulee and submerged the small hill on the left of B. C. Collier's photograph.

Below Saddle Rock

B. C. Collier, ca. 1904   *The Wenatchee World*

465 miles from ocean
778 miles to source

At Entiat Rapids

Unknown photographer, ca. 1950   *The Spokesman-Review*

Entiat Chief Chilcosahskt,
My Great Grandfather

*For many years I traveled the Big River alone in my dugout
canoe. I knew where all the rapids and whirlpools were.
Every year we would catch and dry Salmon to feed us
through the winter. Then I saw my first Suyapenex. He was
a sign of what would come. First, the fur traders, then the
miners, the soldiers and farmers. One day the earth shook, the
big cliff by my home fell across the River, and it ceased to flow.
This was another sign. Soon we Indians were told to move
north. We could no longer follow the game along the river's
shores. My son went but I could not. After me the people saw
the River become a Lake. It too was told to remain in one
spot, just like the Indian.*

—Wendell George

483 miles from ocean
760 miles to source

COLUMBIA RIVER NEAR CHELAN·WASH

Ellis
835

Above Confluence with the Chelan River
Ellis RPPC   Wenatchee Valley Museum & Cultural Center, 005-53-4

505 miles from ocean
738 miles to source

Dutiful

For Warren and Marguerite Ottman

The Okanogan River brings to the Columbia
its last Canadian earth. At this mouth, muddy
and clear waters meet to make this bend a way
of knowing earth is in the current, that eons
of water against farmland and granite made
these dunes, and as the rivers braid at this
last tributary from the blue-rock mountains north
of the border, the sand shows rivers always win.

In a house above this bend, a man and wife
asked for their ashes to be placed apart, though
every night the wife had said, "Don't you ever
leave me." But she wanted to help columbine
and paintbrush color thin earth in July,
and he wanted to be carried by the river
to his birthplace down in Oregon. Dutiful,
their children released the mother's dust
to an alpine meadow in the river's feeding
mountains, and sent the father's light gray body
down among the currents with char and steelhead.
But to make the waiting bearable, the repairing sure,
the sight of father/mother as the other has become,
secure, the hopeful children mixed him up
with her a little, her with him too, like love.

Because this river has the time, it will wash and wash
against the mountains; as the mountains relax
to gravity they will flow back where they arose
from under the ancient sea. And mother and father
again will join, caught up together as their river rests
at last within the ocean's vast approach,
the ocean that (and this the lovers knew for sure),
would come again and receive them to itself.

—Dan Lamberton

Steelhead
Up to 40" – Ocean to below Arrow Lakes (before obstructions)

At Confluence of Okanogan and Columbia Rivers
Werner Langgenhagar, ca.1960   Seattle Public Library

To see to the depth of a river, wade into still water.
In the silent space under the slick of the world, the river
clears. If you stand still too, so as not to wrinkle the water,
you will see the shadows of minnows. You will smell sage
and melting snow and you will notice, incised into the
topography of the silt, little river channels pointing to the sea.
And isn't this what you had hoped to find? A quiet place
where everything comes clear and the earth itself
shows the way to the one thing.

—Kathleen Dean Moore

Stillwater Bay

B. C. Collier, January 1908   NARA Pacific Alaska Region (Seattle), RG77, Portland District

541 miles from ocean
702 miles to source

Old Pierre

You at the tiller, listen, and take in
all that I say–the rudders are your duty;
keep her out of the combers and the smoke;
steer for that headland; watch the drift, or we
fetch up in the smother, and you drown us.
                    ~ *The Odyssey* Book XII, lines 260-265

His old eyes see the headland, know
the river asks and swallows here, billows
and foams; no need for eyes–
ears and his name of rock enough when
forty years before, five friends

      drowned; moss-haired sturgeon pulled them
      down to blindness but floated him,
      rising on a bed frame among ghost-white
      surplice and hymns. His hands oared
      toward the sky, his heart charged

underwater to love these young *kali'tcmen*,
the bright-red kerchiefs tied around
black hair, their muscled backs, the sung
terror of their delight—"Water Monster," he shouts
in the river's tongue. Such music

      collides with voices lost in the grinding
      stream; together the rowers breathe, and
      his mind flows back to lesions
      in wet basalt, to the fine hair
      of infants sprinkled with holy water.

—Jack Johnson

As Long as You Are Human

for Joe Wall, my uncle (1916–1933)

As long as you are human,
you should fear this river.
When you think of it, your nerves
should shrink. In this stone cut
the river is earth's blood—all night
in groan and rush you feel it.
It could exhaust you as it does
the home-sick fish who pound the rocks
with their incessant brains, like imbeciles
who, in the river's suck and cough,
dream the high-flood of disappearing.

The town's newspaper, in each week's issue,
tells of bodies drowned. A cable snapped
and five CCC men gone and never found;
a high-school boy swam to retrieve the grouse
he'd shot, then spun away ten feet from shore;
two woodsmen mangled in their run of logs.

You could be next, with your dainty fly
and rod and claim the river owes you fish
the Indians earned by their own broken spines.

Grand Coulee from Columbia River
Asahel Curtis, ca. 1930   WSHS 34632

Remember how your grandpa choked
to tell you of his girl who climbed high up
a pear tree in her cotton dress, and then looked
down and said to him, "This is as close
to heaven as I will ever be." She drowned
the next day watering her horse.

They keep on grinding down the bedrock
through the nights; two kids found in reeds
a month after a fall, a bloated horse floats past.
The girl's skeleton becomes the river's myth
that means, as she sifts in pieces into sand,
"Don't look for me, I'm never coming back."

—Daniel Lamberton

ASAHEL CURTIS

The Columbia's current forcefully enters two abrupt bends created by rocky outcrops and granite islands that stand in the river's path. The charged water hits the first promontory along the right bank then veers to the left in an abrupt reversal of direction. A drop in the river causes numerous rolling breakers within the rapids. Kettles drilled into the granite rock by the force of the river were shielded from the sun, creating an impression of eye sockets. To Hudson's Bay Company men the site was Hellgate; the Sanpoil Indians fishing along its banks called it "Nxoxoyu," which means "deep eyes."

Hellgate

Frank Palmer, ca. 1910   William Teakle Collection, Northwest Room, Spokane Public Library

619 miles from ocean
624 miles to source

The springtime camp at the confluence of rivers,
known by the descriptive sCmep
and the more loving diminutive ch'ch'map
(both mean "comes to an end"),
was the place to catch suckerfish.
Here, they were cut open and air-dried,
packed for food as the people moved on
to the place of little white camas.

—Gloria Bird

Bridgelip Sucker
Up to 21" – From Cowlitz River to Kootenay River

Longnose Sucker
Up to 25" – Entire River

Largescale Sucker
Up to 20" – Entire River

Confluence of Spokane and Columbia Rivers

Thomas Tolman, ca.1910   Northwest Museum of Arts & Culture, L94-40.80 (retouched)

639 miles from ocean
604 miles to source

On an 1881 army mission to gain knowledge of the upper Columbia, Lieutenant Colonel Thomas W. Symons, cartographer Alfred Downing, and five Indians pushed a weathered Hudson's Bay Company bateaux into the Columbia below Grand Rapids. Riding in front with compass in hand, Downing recorded each bend and drop of the river, noting geographic features as well as adding place names and identifying Indian villages and Chinese mining camps. Twenty miles later the party paddled through the main channel of Turtle Rapid, a short stretch of fast water with a dozen bedrock islands that blocked the river's way.

Neither Symons nor Downing offered any explanation of the rapid's name. We don't know whether it was the site of a mythological event involving Turtle, the outcrops themselves resembled turtles, or whether the crew actually saw turtles sunning themselves on the low rocks that late September afternoon. Aside from a brief mention in the army report, a few photographs and maps provide the only record giving the site distinction. The remaining photographs tell a familiar upper Columbia story; the river's life here is all movement—endless stores of water, boulders, cobbles, and drift pass through carved channels where salmon, sturgeon, suckers, shiners, eels, and other fish make passage.

Turtle Rapid

Frank Palmer. ca. 1910   William Teakle Collection, Northwest Room, Spokane Public Library

673 miles from ocean
570 miles to source

It is difficult to think of the Columbia as simply a river without the history that has grown up around it. In the indigenous worldview the essence of a place and its name were often one. Christine Quintasket (Mourning Dove) and her Salishan relations knew the upper river as "Swa swa netqua" meaning "far-rolling river." In 1792 Captain Robert Grey, after sailing his ship, the *Columbia Rediviva,* across the treacherous sandbars at the river's mouth, christened the river "Columbia," thus linking his discovery to a Spaniard made famous by sailing across the Atlantic to claim North American soils. The renaming brought an identity to the river that would link its future to European notions of ownership and use.

Most early photographs of the Upper Columbia within the United States documented the river's obstructions to one of its potential uses—steamboat navigation. This photograph by Frank Palmer is unusual in that his interest was to record the river's natural beauty by climbing the embankment above Driftwood Island. The driftwood was gone; perhaps swept away by spring floods. At first glance it seems like fog or a low cloud hovers over the island, giving the scene a somewhat otherworldly feel. Closer examination reveals that this is a low part of the island scoured clean by the river. The surviving photograph is unnamed, scratched, and imperfect. We simply view the "far-rolling river."

Driftwood Island

Frank Palmer, ca. 1910   Northwest Museum of Arts & Culture, L84-327.1106 (retouched)

692 miles from ocean
551 miles to source

Rickey Rapids

Here the river should always have a story to tell
   of strong south winds, dark swells blooming among rocks,
pewter clouds hanging over the mountains
   above whirlpools wild and silver as a miner's dream.

Today, as the wind listens to its endless tale,
   the boisterous voice of the river
is reduced to a small rhythm of sorrow,
   a heart pulsing with a long-forgotten purpose
in waves that curl around a rubble of smooth stones.

Geese fly over on dark wings, shadows
   drift and sail like the spirit of what is lost.

      In the silent voice of deep water
      lives the rushing voice of white water,
      the dream voice of water on its way somewhere,
      poised like rain ready to fall,
      aimed like an arrow on a journey to the past.

              —Lynn Rigney Schott

Grand Rapids [Rickey Rapids]

Sxwantitkw

Sxwanitkw   in memory surges   falls downward   releasing glacier   mountain dreams   dances winter spirits   fat with
continuation   completeness   sacred waters touching blue   seeping ice   through tiny streams   pooling into lakes advance through
my mother's childhood   river   changes to thunderous weight leaping   upward swirling   foamy spray misting   gathered salmon
people humming the song of river   rocks moving   the salmon's slow upstream   yearning   toward their mouths swimming in
dark swift currents of life's sweet milk   waterway right   leaving   glassy orange moments waiting   to tumble into the stones
sinuous roll graceful   mystery calling up generations in fluid   coming   home to the people   on the banks moving on   foot
worn stone murmurings of time witnessing   the transformation   into rows of fat   red flesh   fulfilling an old covenant passed

Lower Kettle Falls
Unknown photographer, ca. 1920   Kettle Falls Historical Center

forward twining   future to past   in a time we dream of   now long after   her grandfather's reverent hands   opens the first feast   salmon   while the great mother   river runs free   releasing old salmon   to wash up on the banks   below   the falls long after   she and her grandmother   walk along the pebbly shores   singing   stringing them   through worn and whitened gills   to dry in the wind   on trees   gathering carefully   for hard times   after the last run

—Laxlaxtkw, Jeannette C. Armstrong,
written in the moon of miktuten, sunflower seeds, 2005

Images of Salmon and You

Your absence has left me only fragments of a summer's run
on a night like this, fanning in August heat a seaweeded song.
Sweat glistens on my skin, wears me translucent, sharp as scales

The sun wallowing its giant roe beats my eyes back red and dry.
Have you seen it above the highway ruling you like planets?
Behind you, evening is Columbian, slips dark arms

around the knot of distance that means nothing
to salmon or slim desiring. Sweet man of rivers,
the blood of fishermen and women will drive you back again,

appointed places set in motion like seasons. We are like salmon
swimming against the mutation of current to find
our heartbroken way home again, weight of red eggs and need,

Upper Kettle Falls

Josef Scaylea, ca. 1967   Collection of the Author

Spear Fishing at Lower Kettle Falls

Unknown photographer, undated. William Teakle Collection, Northwest Room, Spokane Public Library.

Sixteen miles below the border, the Columbia suddenly narrows into a *dalle*, the French word that voyageurs coined to describe river channels confined between two steep rocks walls. Typically the water is deep, forming a torrent of extraordinary force and swiftness. Here at The Little Dalles the river fell twenty feet at low water. During the spring freshets, however, the fall lessened as water levels rose a hundred feet along the limestone bluffs.

At the head of the rapids a large reef extended laterally across the current, dividing the river into two powerful currents that sent multiple whirlpools swirling down the narrow canyon. The currents converged a hundred feet downstream into an immense whirlpool capable of swallowing most everything that floated downriver. Observers reported seeing giant cedars taken into the vortex, not to reappear for another mile downstream. Like a frightful being, the maelstrom alternately opened and closed its mouth, making a *whouffing* sound as river debris was sucked into the whirlpool's throat. When it closed, boatmen had a brief opportunity to paddle past the danger—for those whose timing was off, death was a near certainty.

Little Dalles

729 miles from ocean
514 miles to source

International Boundary
to Columbia Lake

River Miles 745 to 1,243

Kokanee (spawning male)
*Up to 20" – Arrow Lakes and
larger lakes in Columbia Basin*

Peamouth
Up to 12" – Entire River

Rainbow Trout (female)
Up to 20" – Entire River

Lake Chub
Up to 6" – Arrow Lakes

Chinook Salmon (spawning male)
Up to 60" – Ocean to Source (before obstructions)

*Eileen Delehanty Pearkes (EDP) gives voice from
Canada to the 280 mile section of river between the
International Boundary and Boat Encampment.*

Shorthead Sculpin
Up to 5" – Canadian Columbia
below Arrow Lakes

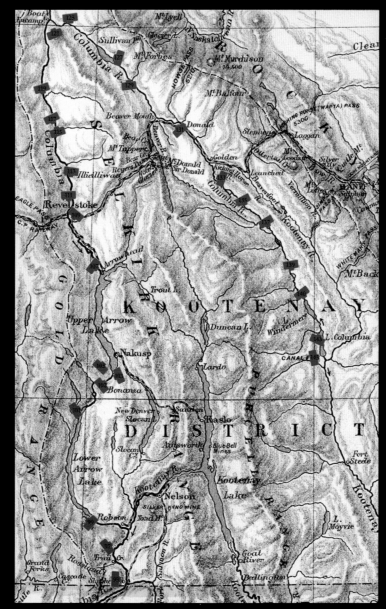

Detail Kootenay District, Edward Stanford   Collection of the Author

Torrent Sculpin
Less than 4" – Entire River

Slimy Sculpin
Less than 4" – Entire Canadian Columbia

Prickly Sculpin
Up to 5" – Estuary up to Arrow Lakes

In response to the Boundary Treaty of 1846, the British Hudson's Bay Company opened Fort Shepherd in 1859 to replace operations at Fort Colville. With only a vague idea of the exact placement of the border at the time, HBC employees took an educated guess when they located the fort. Palliser, an Irish explorer with military training, traveled Western Canada between 1856 and 1859 as leader of the British North America Exploring Expedition.

—EDP

Started before sunrise, and soon turned into the Columbia River. Arrived at Fort Shepherd, near the mouth of the Pendoreille River, and saw where miners had been working for gold, both on the Columbia and on the Pendoreille Rivers. Fort Shepherd is a very well built establishment of the Hudson's Bay Company, but unprotected by pickets. I took an observation here in latitude about 49° 1', and the mouth of Pendoreille River is about three-quarters of a mile within the British territories. While I was observing, a circle of Scotchmen, Americans, and Indians surrounded me, anxiously awaiting my decision as to whether the diggings were in the American Territory or not; strange to say the Americans were quite as much pleased at my pronouncing in favour of Her Majesty, as the Scotchmen; and the Indians began cheering for King George.

—Captain John Palliser, September 4, 1859
The Papers of the Palliser Expedition, 1857-60

Confluence of Pend O'reille and Columbia Rivers

Unknown photographer, Boundary Survey, 1860   U.S. Library of Congress, ppmsca 08567

745.5 miles from ocean
497.5 miles to source

The Sovereign River

The river has entered a kingdom ruled by high mountains,
monarchs on granite thrones, crowned in glistening ice.
Forested capes sweep down to the valleys
where deep shadows darken the velvet folds
and mock the passing sun.

The reign of these mountains has been so brief.
The river rushes to overtake them,
to smooth them with her sweet water,
and strip them of their ermine grandeur.

Just to prove
      that sovereignty only asserts domain
      while a more essential vigor passes across unseen boundaries.

The form of a river,
malleable and yet certain.

Blue are these mountains
merely.

—Eileen Delehanty Pearkes

The Columbia pauses as all rivers do. In the 150 miles from Galena Bay to Castlegar, it declines only twelve feet, forming two long, deep bowls, the Lower and Upper Arrow Lakes. As the river widens twice, the current nearly disappears, sinking its heavy head into the pillow of landscape. The juvenile sockeye who have not yet journeyed to the ocean circle around the returning chinook in the cool darkness, perhaps sensing the ocean brine still clinging to the skin of the dying fish. Having been slowed by many falls and pushed against many rapids, the chinook make good time in the quiet water. We cannot know for certain whether they feel relief, or whether they simply push through the predictable calm. Nor can we possibly understand how the fish might anticipate the sequence of steeply ascending rapids that lie ahead. Do they smell the turbulence that awaits them, or feel its reverberations with their fins? Instinct may be a sort of knowingness, an awareness that cannot be measured.

—EDP

Juvenile Sockeye Salmon
Up to 20″ – Arrow Lakes to Ocean (before obstructions)

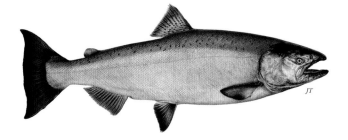

Chinook Salmon
Up to 60″ – Entire River (before obstructions)

South End of Lower Arrow Lake

Wm. Notman & Sons, 1903   McCord Museum, View 3675 (retouched)

794 miles from ocean
449 miles to source

Waiting for Coyote's Return

i have always been told to wait for Coyote's return.
i used to wonder . . . what does that mean?
i begin to understand now
as i realize that my people have endured
a season of extinction.
Memories stolen and . . . hidden now . . . in lies . . .
and then flooded
And. . . that was the mistake.

The memories are beginning to come alive
and the water calls to me.
i go to this place in the river
and pour the water over me.
Water gives birth to memories . . .
to life . . . to love. i pour the water over me
and as the water washes down my face
it traces another memory there.

the water fills my eyes with the past
and i look up from the river and see—
there sits the old Auntie . . . Anne. . .
thinking about her love . . . over there.
She looks at this water . . . knowing the love . . .
Coyote's love . . . made all this . . . even her.
But she could not succumb to her love . . .
she. . . must hold the memory.
She would succumb to death though and
her death would mark her people . . . She knew
Coyote would not be back in her lifetime . . .
she knew . . . she must hold the memory.

i am the old Auntie now . . . holding to the memory.
Waiting . . . in my life time? . . . i don't know . . . probably not.
Coyote gave us to the river . . . an expression of love.
Coyote will make it right.
Bringing back to love,
        bringing back another memory.
We're all waiting here,
    awash with those memories.
        We sit with the bones in the water,
            waiting for the memories,
                waiting to be again,
                    waiting for coyote.
In my lifetime? . . . i don't know . . . probably not.

—marilyn james

Oatescott and Columbia River

Hans Leu, ca. 1950   Karl Krey Collection

831 miles from ocean
412 miles to source

Goose Island

Hans Leu, ca. 1950   Karl Krey Collection

Between the two sapphire lakes, the Columbia forms
a twenty-six-mile chain of smaller jewels, linked by the
glitter of water. In the Narrows, current sparkles along the
twisting shoreline. Marshlands of reed canary grass and
sedge absorb the annual freshet like a breath being deeply
inhaled. Dense gatherings of cottonwood and birch crowd
the littoral, giving way higher up to cedar, hemlock, pine
and fir, forests that moan quietly in the changeable winds.
Sand and gravel bars part themselves around Goose
Island, Sand Island, Swan Island, and the Dispatch Islands.
Sometimes, sturgeon wallow along the crystalline shore,
turning their white skin toward the summer sun. Osprey
nest on bleached cottonwood spars. Songbirds cavort in
the leafy tangle below. An elegant sturgeon-nosed canoe,
a voyageur's bateau, a stately steamboat, all carve their
paddles into a mountain reflected by the shining stillness
of water. Stronger than stone, the river shifts what seems
immovable. It makes transparent even the density of time.

—EDP

839 miles from ocean
404 miles from source

The Narrows

Hans Leu, ca. 1950   Karl Krey Collection

841 miles from ocean
402 miles to source

In the fall of 1847, the Canadian traveling artist Paul Kane paddled north from Fort Colville at Kettle Falls. His record of passing through the valley of the Lower and Upper Arrow Lakes is a rare, detailed account of the striking expanse of water and mountain, by this time only sparsely populated with Sinixt people due to the effects of multiple devastating epidemics and the draw of Fort Colville.

—EDP

Sept. 26th— It continued raining heavily all night, and heavy mists hung over us during the day; but we continued our journey and got into what is called another lake.
Sept. 27th— Still in the lakes. The day was clearer, and we could distinguish the surrounding scenery, which seemed to consist of immense mountains, towering peak on peak above the clouds. . . . The cedars are of enormous magnitude, some of them measuring not less than thirty or forty feet in circumference. I was told of one fifty feet, but did not see it. I attempted to reach the upper side of one which had been uprooted and lay on the ground, with the end of my gun stretched out at arm's length, and could but just attain it.
Sept. 28th— We had an exciting chase after a mountain goat, which showed himself in the distance, on a point of land jutting out into the lake. Putting the boat ashore, I started in pursuit, accompanied by three or four Indians, and after a long hunt succeeded in killing him. He afforded us a most delicious repast. . . .

—Paul Kane
Wanderings of an Artist Among the Indians of North America

Upper Arrow Lake from Mountain Meadow

Hans Leu, ca. 1950   Karl Krey Collection

862 miles to from ocean
381 miles to source

At a place the Sinixt call *kwespits'a7* [Buffalo Robe], the lake becomes river again, cresting and ebbing around a small island of cottonwoods while the current swells over gravel bars littered with chinook spawn. The name hints at the exchange long ago of salmon for the hides of an animal foreign to mountains, or of dried berries for sweetgrass, a plant that sways in a different wind. The Sinixt trade with their neighbours—the Ktunaxa, Secwepemc, and Okanagan—all along the valley, linking the river with oceans of grass or sage that lie beyond the mountains.

In 1838 the "black robes" arrive. Fathers Blanchet and Demers offer mass in the village, opening their arms to the splendid view. By 1900 the railway coming south from Revelstoke has reached the place settlers have named "Arowhead," for the scores of stone tools they found scattered on the shore. Docks host boats from the Columbia & Kootenay Steam Navigation Company. In the following decades, mills, wharves, booms, railways, and boathouses convert the trade of buffalo robes, salmon, and arrowheads into the business of forestry, mining, and agriculture. Eventually, the commerce of water converts the natural river and lakeshore of the valley into a reservoir, submersing salmon redds, places for sturgeon to wallow, ancestral villages, burials, islands, townsites, and numerous family-farms.*

—EDP

North End of Upper Arrow Lake

Unknown photographer, unknown date   British Columbia Archives, D-02686

892 miles from ocean
351 miles to source

The valley between the Selkirk and Monashee mountains grows more confined, and the river follows suit. In the minds of fur traders, miners, and early settlers, the Columbia becomes at once rude, uncooperative, dangerous, and foreboding. Between Big Eddy and Boat Encampment, seven sets of rapids tangle the passage of water, and several canyons compress its flow into a 403 feet elevation change in ninety-two miles. Upstream travel now involves intense physical struggle with lines and poles. Moving downstream, river travelers hope for the best as boats tip, sway, and sometimes upturn. For its part, the river does not understand inhospitability and disfavor. It knows only the mystery of being water, compounded and intensified as peaks rise with greater certainty toward the sky.

—EDP

Big Eddy with Mount Begbie

Charles S. Bailey, ca. 1890   City of Vancouver Archives, SQN 234

933 miles from ocean
310 miles to source

The Columbia finds passage the only way it can through such a tangled yet firm geography, as grace links arms with beauty to display the essential nature of moving water. Dancing with soft feet across hard cobbles, the river swirls effortlessly around fixed objects. Rapids of white lace trim the river's smooth, liquid skirts, and a passing wind ripples its glistening tresses. On such a day, the river moves with flexible joy, as the gentle music of water-laughter rises through the canyon. On other days, when melting snows or brash spring rains surge into the channel, an urgent roar drowns out the laughter, filling the air with a mixture of awe and fear.

—EDP

Steamboat Rapids

R. H. Truman & Co., 1904   City of Vancouver Archives, CVA 2-93

934 miles from ocean
309 miles to source

The River's Hands

Light captures silt carried down from glacial plains,
where it transforms into the many colours of water:
cerulean
icy green
cobalt
turquoise
milky aqua
rushing ultramarine.

Hue of ice.
The move from solid
to liquid
to an unspeakable vision
suspended in the depths of certainty.

Silken skeins of light hang in the current,
waiting
to be woven
by the river's hands.

—Eileen Delehanty Pearkes

Pygmy Whitefish
Less than 6" – Canadian Columbia and
deeper lakes of the Columbia Basin

Mountain Whitefish
Up to 21" – Entire River

Frenchman's Cap

Nicholas Morant, ca. 1947   Canadian Pacific Railway Archives, M4214

In the Hand of Catherine:
A Columbia River Journey   October 24, 1838

When the river took the blessings of Catherine Roussil-
Chalifoux-Comartin
Larch votives flamed on forested banks
And dusk shrouded the dangerous rapids.

We were 26 with some freight, too many for one boat.

The river knew nothing of the wet furs,
the anxious passengers, the weight of a mother's love.

The boatmen were fighting to bring us ashore
when Mr. Wallace, one of the Englishmen,
stood up and took his wife in his arms.

and the canoe turned its belly to the dim light.

Fast rushing water
A lumbering hulk
Packs of freight
Struggling bodies
Cold, cold water

Sodden passengers slogged to dry land
weeping, without Catherine's two children of the river

I was too stunned to feel anything right then...
my baby, dead at 24 days, as well as Charles,
first son and his grandfathers' namesake.

The river offered no invocation for the baptism,
roaring through cathedral walls,
scraping its quick current against the canyon,
pulling the infant into its churning font,
trapping the toddler in the cave of the upturned boat.

Just three children were found: Charles
and the two Leblancs, Pierre and Rose.
All three were buried by a wooden
cross at House of the Lakes.

Catherine bound her swelling breasts and continued
south. The boat swayed in the current as she counted beads
of nothingness, her rosary of grief.

This, an account of the river's libation.

—Eileen Delehanty Pearkes
The Hand of Catherine, Columbia's DaughterCatherine
Roussil-Chalifoux-Comartin by George Thomas Brown.

Priest Rapids

Narrow as a needle, the river threads through impermeable rock outcroppings that confine it beyond all civility. Foaming water and brooding shadows expose the river's uncooperative spirit, its inexplicable wrath. A nearly perpendicular shelf of rock on one side of the channel pushes against the water, boiling it up into a froth that continues for over forty yards below the rapids themselves. The only possible safe passage for any bateau, barge, or canoe exists on the opposite shore, where a craft must pass through the eye of the needle in order to avoid being chewed up by the rocky rapids. Some boats succeed in this challenge and others do not, the unlucky ones emerging from the rapids tattered beyond all meaning, battered, or lost. By 1850 Les Dalles des Morts [Death Rapids] has a deserved reputation as one of the most dangerous places on the entire Columbia.

—EDP

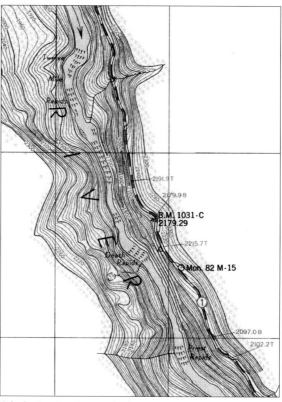

Columbia River Basin Survey, 1948, Sheet 27   Fort Steele Heritage Town Archives

Les Dalles des Morts [Death Rapids]

Earle Dickey, ca. 1945   British Columbia Archives, F-05897

972 miles from ocean
271 miles from source

Into the Unknown (1856–1865)

How the miners travel with such earnestness toward their search,
boats poling through rapids,
boots splitting from the wetting, weight of snow.

Gold has a way of causing an ache in a man's heart. Call it greed
or curiosity
or an urge to transform.

Goldstream, French, Cairne—
dozens of claims on the three richest streams.

They sift the glacial silt and sand, search the rubble,
sluice the spring melt as it surges.
They are obsessed like the ancient alchemist,
the wizard who combined base metals, air and water
who used vials and beakers, fires and burners.

The miners work with frenzy,
surrounded by pitched bedrock and bouldered channels. They yearn
for the precious weight of being,
for the gold
hidden
in the rushing water.

—Eileen Delehanty Pearkes

Explorer and cartographer David Thompson and botanist David Douglas each traveled the rugged upper Columbia River in the early 19th century. In the winter of 1810–11, Thompson constructed a boat of cedar planks at the confluence of the Canoe, Wood, and Columbia, a place he called Boat Encampment. Today, stumps from the magnificent forests of Big Bend hover beneath the water of the Kinbasket reservoir while the words of the two men rise to the surface.

—EDP

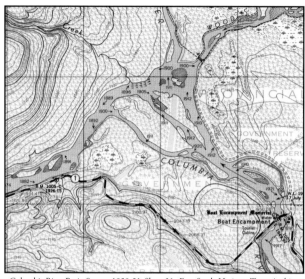

Columbia River Basin Survey, 1950-51, Sheet 31   Fort Steele Heritage Town Archives

Douglas: . . . *at a short turn of the river one of the most magnificent prospects in Nature opened to our view. The daily wished for dividing-ridge of the continent, bearing north-east, distance six miles. The sight of the mountains is most impressive. Their height . . . from 6000 to 6500 feet, two-thirds covered with wood. . . .*

Thompson: *These two streams [the Wood and Canoe Rivers] . . . formed a wide alluvial, on which are forest Trees of enormous size; the white Cedars . . . from 15 to 36 feet girth; clean grown and tall in proportion. . . . The pines . . . from 18 to 42 feet in girth, measured at 10 feet above the ground, which the snow enabled us to do. . . . They were finely formed and rose full 200 feet without a branch, and threw off very luxuriant heads. The white birch was also a stately Tree, tall and erect. . . .*

Douglas: *Although I have been travelling for the last fifteen days surrounded by high snowy mountains, and the eye has become familiar to them and apt to lose that exalted idea of their magnitude, yet on beholding those mentioned impresses on the mind a feeling beyond what I can express. . . .*

Thompson: *On the east side of the Mountains the Trees were small, a stunted growth with branches to the ground; there we were Men, but on the west side we were pigmies; in such forests what could we do with Axes of two pound weight.*

David Thompson's Narrative of His Explorations in Western America, 1784–1812
Journal Kept by David Douglas during His Travels in North America, 1823–1827

Boat Encampment at the Big Bend

Rey Marr, 1947   Whyte Museum of the Canadian Rockies, V761/1PA

1,025 miles from ocean
218 miles to source

Your choice was always clear: not the long struggle
Upstream against the current, against the constant
Headlong pummeling of snow-melt and downpour
Nor the leaf-slow easy drifting
Downstream, the way all trees on a cutbank bend
Before they fall, but simply staying
Here by the river where you watch and wait
For what appears, moves past, and vanishes.

You've learned what you can about this watery sky,
Its rearrangement of your slight reflections,
Its turmoil, each moment so subtly various,
You can hardly tell, can hardly remember
What you marveled over only a glance before:
The shimmering, the lovely formalities
Of a chaos you can touch with your finger-ends,
A surface whose tarnished and burnished galaxies
Are born and borne away, but instantly
Return in a translucent blossoming.

You know under that surface always, no matter
What may seem apparent by sunlight,
Cloudlight, or moonlight, another life is passing,
Not just the stones and snags, the common bed-load
Of all rivers, not only the star-backed swimmers
Whose falls and springs once dazzled you into believing
You could dream your way to the source, but the Other

Whose body is never still, is always turning
Away from you downriver as if to stream
To an end beyond you through the deepest channels,
And yet remains beside you, whose light is lighter
Than air, whose breath is water, whose water is light.

—David Wagoner

Confluence of Canoe, Wood and Columbia Rivers
R. M. Patterson, 1947   Patterson Family Collection

Sixty-eight-year-old river explorer M. J. Lorraine built a small boat at Canal Flats in 1921 and proceeded to row the entire length of the river to Astoria. Strong and compact, he was a man with a feisty disposition, ideally suited to the river's magnificent challenges. His highly detailed descriptions of the river offer an intimate view that permits the reader to join the excitement. He provides the following overview of eighteen miles of rugged river between Boat Encampment and Kinbasket Lake, where the water drops more than fourteen feet per mile.

Between Kinbasket Lake and the Ferry (at Boat Encampment) there are fifteen separate rapids. . . . I consider Kinbasket, or Twenty-three Mile Rapids, at time of high water, the most trying section to navigate of the whole Columbia River. Not because they are the roughest— although they are rough enough in places—but because of their length and continuity. They are the longest on the River, the next being Priest Rapids, in the United States, but which do not compare with them for violence. . . . The rapids are caused by either submerged or protruding rocks over or against which the swiftly moving water dashes and throws upward great froth-topped waves, breakers, or combers.

—M. J. Lorraine

Between Boat Encampment and Kinbasket Lake

Unknown photographer, undated   British Columbia Archives, A-09305

1,025–1,050 miles to ocean
218–193 miles to source

Breaking Trail on Upper Columbia River
A. A. McCoubrey, ca. 1907   Victoria University (Toronto)

To experience the remote beauty of Kinbasket Lake in the early days required willingness to brave a long series of rapids that exist on both approaches to the lake. For those who took the risk, or for those who traveled to visit the lake after the Big Bend Highway opened in 1940, the scenic rewards were ample. On a still summer day they viewed glaciers of Mount Trident rising four thousand feet to the west, and to the east, the spine of the Canadian Rockies, rising even higher.

David Thompson had no praise when he came upon the frozen lake in the early spring of 1811. Everything was snow-blindingly bright with no game or good places to camp. Thompson's men had no alternative but to drag their heavy cedar boat across more than seven miles of snow-bound lake. Upon reaching the open water of the inlet, hunter René Vallade finally discovered two newly nested swans, their first fresh food in days. Thompson's words give no acknowledgment to the beauty of Kinbasket's winter—his only focus was the inner landscape, which was anything but pleasant: "We all wet and sadly benumbed."

Kinbasket Lake

BC Government, 1957   British Columbia Archives, I-21408

1,051 miles to ocean
192 miles to source

Surprise Rapids as Described by Rivermen

an onslaught of light / and sound
builds to earth shaking / throbs and rumbles /
below the higher / roar of dancing water

a savage stretch of foam / white water
falls in a roaring cascade /
and disappears into / the whirlpool's waiting maw

black tips of jutting bedrock appear /
the river bends sharply / to the left

beyond a sentinel island /
the river rushes / into the rapid's final descent
high rolling billows / form curling waves

—Gathered Words from
M. J. Lorraine, *The Columbia Unveiled*
A.P. Coleman, *The Canadian Rockies*

Columbia River Basin Survey, 1950-51, Sheet 35   Fort Steele Heritage Town Archives

We plunged into a sheer-walled chute that led to the first series of curves, the river climbing against the outside of turns and leaving the inside bends to lower suckholes and boils around jutting rocks. We knifed through the curve by the railroad tracks, nudging the waterbillow of a mid-river boulder and slam-dancing another, and then into a series of standing waves—Kitchen Rapids. The river narrowed, and we blasted these breakers head-on. The boat rose high on the crest of each wave and then pitched down to smack the next one. Angry water broke across the bow, over which I registered nothing but sky, water, sky, water, in rapid sequence. We slid backward, then sideways, into a suckhole. The river in the voice of God said, "You're mine." And our little craft answered, "No we're not. . . ." The Columbia River barreled past. I left my body for a while to watch this from a neutral tree branch, just to see how it would all come out, but the suckhole reversed itself into a rising pillow, as a suckhole will, and tossed us forward toward a final set of curves where we glided out into the calm open headwaters of Kinbasket.

—Robin Cody

Redgrave Canyon

O. B. Buell, 1885   Glenbow Archives, NA-3188-17

1,106 miles to ocean
137 miles to source

From the silent winter come whispers of spring—suddenly out of southern skies a wild *kow-wowing* of a thousand tundra swans signals the return of birds to the wetlands of the Columbia. More than two hundred species of varying sizes and persuasions travel the unseen river of air. Many stop to gather strength for their journey north. Others— the divers, daubers, tree sitters, the woodpeckers, and those with pointed beaks and stilty legs—arrive to nest. Decked in showy strips of plumage or disguised to blend into backgrounds, the birds busy themselves with feeding, courting, and song.

While awaiting a mate, a marsh wren perched on cattails and reeds proclaims to all that this is his territory. Hearing the male's colorful song, a newly arrived female pays a visit. After a flurry of introductions, he shows her several nests that he has intricately woven from strips of pliable cattail leaves, grasses, and stems. If the female accepts, she will add more leaves, stems, rootlets, and the fluff of cattails or feathers to line the nest's bottom. The half dozen chicks that soon emerge from delicate shells will spend their first twelve days cradled in a nest that sways to movements of wind. Wetland insects and spiders, some of whom climb the very stalks upon which the nests are built, provide a steady source of food. After peeking out from a small opening in the nest, the fledglings fly into the world's fullness while the adult marsh wren darts furtively among the bushes and reeds, singing a melodic repertoire of over two hundred songs.

As Though the Word Blue Had Been Dropped into the Water

The running stream
   is fragrant.

On the bank, in the shadows,
a small yellow flower
   with sunlight at its feet
puts my life together.

The little bird that is
   going to heal me
is hopping around in the bushes.

—Robert Sund

Columbia River near Canyon Creek

Unknown photograper, ca. 1955   British Columbia Archives, D-02829

1,136 miles from ocean
107 miles to source

Climbing along the River

Willows never forget how it feels
to be young.

Do you remember where you came from?
Gravel remembers.

Even the upper end of the river
believes in the ocean

Exactly at midnight
yesterday sighs away.

What I believe is,
all animals have one soul.

Over the land they love
they crisscross forever.

—William Stafford

30 Miles South of Golden

H. W. Gleason, July 15, 1912   Glenbow Archives, NC-53-204

The meandering river near its source follows the Rocky Mountain Trench, formed eons ago and given present shape and substance by the last great glaciers. Eighty streams continually bring loads of silt and gravel that create terraces, scarps, and alluvial fans adjacent to the main river channel. The wetlands are a thousand fluid twists and turns, set off by shallow ponds of open water, the whole providing lush habitat for deer, elk, moose, martin, beaver, coyote, wolves, and others. Those flying overhead might think the river a liquid braid lined with birches, willows, sedges, grasses, rushes, and reeds. The long, narrow expanse of water absorbs and filters moisture, reduces floods, and eases drought, all the while providing numerous niches and habitats for a thriving array of plants, birds, fish, and animals that live within this remarkable setting of snow-capped mountains rising directly from the valley floor. One of the longest continuous wetlands in North America, much of the area is now under the protection of the Columbia Wetlands Wildlife Reserve.

Where Winter Burbot Roil

Where winter burbot roil
a heron stands
thin as rushes
a patient hunter
still life

—Peter Christensen

Burbot
Up to 30" – Wenatchee River to Lake Windermere
and larger Lakes of the Canadian Basin

Near Spillimacheen

R. M. Patterson, 1940   Patterson Family Collection

1,179 miles from ocean
64 miles to source

Salmon's Return

for *Oncorhynchus tshawytscha*

Sleek-bodied resolution has met fast water,
   raced canyons and leapt falls
      to these precise gravels.

Battered, weak, and covered with sores,
   one fish is minus an eye,
      another its lower jaw.

At the river's end
   stones and pebbles receive bright eggs
      showered in clouds of sperm

   as osprey, people, and bear
      wait for flashing fins
         rippling across the river.

—William Layman

Looking toward the Purcells near Radium Hot Springs

H. W. Gleason, September 18, 1914   Glenbow Archives NC 53-278

Somewhere In the Heavens

As cold and warm air kiss
winds thrust clouds
among jagged rocks

somewhere in the heavens
a river begins

water cuts
the crust of the earth
fractures light

Outlet of Lake Windermere

H. W. Gleason, September 16, 1909   Glenbow Archives, NC-53-564

Lake Windermere

Hoodoos from Columbia Lake
William Layman, 2003   Collection of the Author

When David Thompson made first contact with the valley's inhabitants, he learned that the Ktunaxa spoke a unique language and had lived in the Columbia Valley for many years. Their descendants, the Two Lakes people of the Columbia Lake Band, continue to live on a reserve along the shore of Lake Windermere, as do the more recently arrived Kinbasket Band, whose reserve is adjacent to the river below its outlet with Lake Windermere. Ktunaxa oral tradition tells that their people were created out of the blood spilled from the body of an immense salmon that traveled through the Rocky Mountain Trench in the time of the spirit world. The Hoodoos that rise spectacularly from the outlet of Dutch Creek are the bones of that great fish.

Columbia Lake Cooking North
Unknown photographer, undated   Fort Steele Heritage Town Archives, FS 72.135

1,235 miles to ocean
8 miles from source

The Columbia originates from numerous springs found in the shallow waters near the southern shore of Columbia Lake. Some people, however, have registered disagreement that the lake is the river's true source. British climber J. Norman Collie believed that such a great river deserved better than to begin as a lowly swamp, so he declared the Columbia Icefields to be the place where the river begins. In 1921 river adventurer Lewis Freeman also questioned the location of the Columbia's first waters. He judged that if the source of a river begins at the place where water travels the greatest distance to reach the river's mouth, then Dutch Creek should hold the distinction, as its grey-green glacial waters travel 28 miles before giving its waters to Columbia Lake near the lake's outlet. Yet government and tradition have followed the lead of David Thompson, the first officially to identify Columbia Lake as the river's source. The surrounding mountains provide a fitting element of grandeur that contributes to a collective sense that from this place a great river begins.

On the 14th, we came to the head of the Columbia River 268 miles from our winter Hut. I could never pass this singular place without admiring its situation, and romantic bold scenery; . . . other Rivers have their sources so ramified in Rills and Brooks that it is not easy to determine the parent stream, this is not the case with the Columbia River, near the foot of a steep secondary mountain, surrounded by a fine grassy Plain, lies its source, in a fine Lake of about eleven square miles of area, from which issues its wild rapid Stream, yet navigable to the sea.

—David Thompson
David Thompson's Narrative, May 14th, 1811

Nose Hill on Columbia Lake

H. W. Gleason, August 6, 1912   Glenbow Archives, NC-53-255

1,243 miles to ocean

Contributors

Linda Andrews's first book of poetry, *Escape of the Bird Woman,* won the Washington State Governor's Award in 1999. Andrews also has received numerous citations for poetry, including the Richard Blessing Award from the University of Washington. She lives in Walla Walla, Washington, where she teaches at Walla Walla Community College.

Jeannette Armstrong (Penticton Band of the Okanagan) is a Canadian author and activist whose lifework and writings have won numerous awards, including the 2003 EcoTrust Buffet Award for Indigenous Leadership and the 2005 Angel Award. She is director of the En'owkin International School of Writing in Penticton.

Gloria Bird (Spokane Tribe) is the author of *Full Moon on the Reservation* (1993) and *The River of History* (1997). She also co-edited *Reinventing the Enemy's Language* (1997) with Joy Harjo. She lives and works on the Spokane Indian Reservation in Washington State.

Peter Christensen, poet, writer, singer-songwriter, works seasonally as a park ranger in British Columbia's wild north-west. He has published four books and has contributed to numerous anthologies, writing journals, and magazines in both the United States and Canada.

Robin Cody is the author of *Ricochet River* (1992) and *Voyage of the Summer Sun* (1995), winner of the Oregon Book Award and the Pacific Northwest Booksellers Association Award. He lives with his wife, Donna, in Portland.

Wendell George (Colville Confederated Tribes) returned to the Colville Reservation after a fifteen-year career with Boeing. He has served his tribe as a councilman, CEO of their enterprises, and trustee for Wenatchee Valley College. He lives in Omak with his wife, Barbara.

marilyn james is the appointed spokesperson of the Sinixt Nation, an aboriginal group declared extinct by the federal government of Canada in 1956. marilyn is also the aboriginal advisor at Selkirk college and holds a masters degree in education from Simon Fraser University.

Jack Johnson, a poet, cemetery sexton, stone mason, and occasional officiate, teaches writing and literature at Wenatchee Valley College. A native of Peshastin, Washington, he has long had a fascination with the area's rich natural and human history.

Dan Lamberton grew up on his family's farm above the Okanogan and Columbia Rivers. He now lives in Walla Walla, Washington, where he is director of the Humanities Program at Walla Walla College.

William Layman was awarded the James B. Castles Award in 1997 for contributions to a deeper understanding of the Columbia River's heritage. Author of *Native River: The Columbia Remembered* (WSU Press, 2002), he writes history, directs a community theatre company, and is a research associate for the Royal British Columbia Museum.

C. Dan McConnell, certified scientific illustrator, is a lifelong resident of Washington. Born in Chelan, raised in Quincy, Dan has lived on an orchard south of Dryden for 30 years. He has drawn, painted, sculpted, and cartooned since childhood.

Tim McNulty is a poet, essayist, environmental activist, educator, and nature writer. He is the author of two collections of poetry and ten books on natural history and conservation. He lives with his wife and daughter in the foothills of the Olympic Mountains.

Kathleen Dean Moore is best known for her award-winning books about rivers and the sea. She is Distinguished Professor of Philosophy at Oregon State University, where she directs the Spring Creek Project for Ideas, Nature, and the Written Word.

Eileen Delehanty Pearkes lives and writes in the landscape of the Upper Columbia River, at Nelson, British Columbia. She has published numerous essays on landscape and the imagination and is author of *The Geography of Memory* and *Heart of the River*, and co-author of *The Inner Green.*

Theodore Roethke (1908-1963), known for his poetic explorations of nature within a regional setting, is regarded as one of the most influential American poets of the 20th century. He is author of six books of poems, including *The Waking,* winner of the Pulitzer Prize for poetry in 1954.

Lynn Rigney Schott teaches English at Kettle Falls High School. A strong love of living along the Columbia has inspired her writing for many years. Her work appears in numerous literary magazines and anthologies.

Derek Sheffield lives in the foothills of the Cascades where Eagle Creek winds toward the Columbia. He teaches English at Wenatchee Valley College. Blue Begonia Press published his chapbook of poems, *A Mouthpiece of Thumbs* (2000), and in 2004, he was awarded an Artist Trust GAP Grant.

Kim Stafford, director of Lewis & Clark College's Northwest Writing Institute, writes books of prose and poetry that highlight the wonder of local discoveries within the larger story of human experience. Winner of a Citation for Excellence from the Western States Book Awards in 1986, Stafford lives in Portland with his wife and children.

William Stafford (1914-1993) published sixty books of poetry and prose in his lifetime and, yet, "would trade everything I ever wrote for the next thing." He was a lifelong witness for reconciliation with the earth, people, and the self.

Robert Sund's love of words, poetry and place, his playful nature, and his keen aesthetic sense have come together in a posthumous publication, *Poems from Ish River Country.*

Terry Toedtemeier is the curator of photography for the Portland Art Museum, where he has built a collection of over 5,000 images that trace the medium's history from the age of the daguerreotype to the present. He has specialized in the history of photography in the Columbia River Gorge and the work of Carleton Watkins.

Joseph Tomelleri's illustrations of fish have earned him world-wide recognition as an artist who combines beauty and scientific accuracy. Known for his exquisite attention to detail and unparalleled mastery of color, his artwork has appeared in numerous books and publications throughout the United States and Mexico.

David Wagoner has published seventeen books of poems, most recently, *Good Morning and Good Night* (2005), and ten novels, one of which, *The Escape Artist*, was made into a movie by Francis Ford Coppola. He edited *Poetry Northwest* for the University of Washington until its end in 2002.

Terri White, exhibits curator for the Wenatchee Valley Museum & Cultural Center, combines a long standing interest in natural history and art with her expertise as a professional exhibit designer for *River of Memory: The Everlasting Columbia,* as well as other exhibits.

Elizabeth Woody (Millee-thlama/Wyampum/Tly-til-pum/ Wasco-Wish-Xam-Watlalla/Hawaiian/Dine/ 1/32 other) is recipient of the 1990 American Book Award, Hedgebrook's J. T. Stewart Award, and PNBA's discretional William Stafford Memorial Award for Poetry.

Susan Zwinger lives on an island off the coast of Washington, where she has just completed her fifth book, *The Hanford Reach: The Arid Lands of South Central Washington.* Her work combines her passions for the natural world with her talents as teacher, writer, and artist.

Credits

"Conversion," Elizabeth Woody, from *First Fish: First People*, with permission of University of Washington Press, Seattle, Washington, 1999.

"The Rose," copyright 1963 by Beatrice Roethke, administratrix of the Estate of Theodore Roethke, from *The Collected Poems of Theodore Roethke* by Theodore Roethke. Used by permission of Doubleday, a division of Random House, Inc.

"Recognition of the Maker," copyright 2004, from *Conversion: Root, Stone, Flesh, and Water*, a CD by Elizabeth Woody. Used by permission of the author.

Quote of Earl Roberge from *Columbia: The Great River of the West*, copyright 1985, Chronicle Books, San Francisco, CA.

"Ask Me" and "Climbing along the River," copyright 1977, 1991, 1998 by the Estate of William Stafford. Reprinted from *The Way It Is: New & Selected Poems*, with the permission of Graywolf Press, Saint Paul, Minnesota.

Passages of Robin Cody adapted from *Voyage of a Summer Sun: Canoeing the Columbia River*, 1995. Used by permission of the author.

"By a River," David Wagoner, from *Traveling Light: Collected and New Poem*, copyright 1999 by David Wagoner. Used with permission of the author and the University of Illinois Press.

"As Though the Word Blue Had Been Dropped into the Water," copyright Robert Sund Poets House Trust. Reprinted from *Poems from Ish River Country*, with permission of Shoemaker & Hoard, Publishers, Emeryville, California, 2004."

"Images of Salmon and You" from *Full Moon on the Reservation*. New York: The Greenfield Review Press. Copyright 1993 by Gloria Bird. Reprinted by permission of the author and Greenfield Review Press.

Quote of Paul Kane from *Paul Kane's Frontier,* copyright 1971. Used by permission of Amon Carter Museum, Fort Worth, Texas.

"Where Winter Burbot Roil" and "Somewhere in the Heavens" are used by permission of the author.

Fish illustrations are copyrighted and used by permission of the contributing artists.

Map of Columbia Basin. Cartography by the King County GIS Center (www.metrokc.gov/gis). Copyright Wenatchee Valley Museum & Cultural Center, Wenatchee, Washington. Depiction of the freshwater plumes of the Columbia River from Barnes, Duxbury, and Morse in chapter 3 of *The Columbia River Estuary and Adjacent Ocean Waters*, 1972, University of Washington Press.

Acknowledgments

The Wenatchee Valley Museum & Cultural Center is a partnership between the City of Wenatchee and the WVMCC Association, whose mission is to gather and educate people to celebrate and preserve the history, arts, sciences, and rich diversity of north central Washington. Upon hearing of the project, the city and the museum board enthusiastically endorsed both the exhibition and book. Museum Director Keith Williams has been steadfast in his belief that the project be realized to the fullest extent, while Exhibits Curator Terri White has provided her keen insights and aesthetic sensibilities.

The web of relationships supporting the author's Columbia River work has shaped the project's life over many years. In 1975 James Donaldson of Twisp, Washington, brought carefully tended embers to a community within north central Washington that has kept the fire of bioregionalism alive. David Nicandri of the Washington State Historical Society, William Lang, and the late John Brown added energy to the work's circle of support along the way. The consistent spiritual guidance of Rex Buck and the Wanapums has added immeasurable depth to both the research and outcomes of this project.

A special thanks to Joseph Tomelleri and Dan McConnell who graciously allowed us to use their many fine fish illustrations; to Blythe Whitely and Chuck Peven for teaching volunteer artists to create silk renderings of the native fish for the exhibition; to Kim Stafford, Elizabeth Woody, and Dan Lamberton for guidance with various poetic elements of the exhibit; and to Eileen Delehanty Pearkes for writing eloquently of the 280-mile stretch of river north of the border. To each contributing writer, poet, and illustrator: know that our museum is deeply grateful for the beautiful way in which everyone responded. Thanks as well to composer, producer Lynette Westendorf along with Tanya Lawson, Kara Hunnicutt, Michael Conrad, Tim Brooks, and Terry Hunt, who shared their remarkable musical talent, and to Malcolm Keithley for assistance with creating the exhibit's excellent soundtrack. The companion CD of music, poetry, and natural sounds provides to the ear what the exhibit gives to the eyes. Special mention also goes to cartographer Patrick Jankanish who created the map of our dreams.

More than thirty different museums, archives, libraries, newspapers, agencies, and individuals contributed to this book. In each case, doors were opened widely to locate and make available material from their collections. A special acknowledgment is due to Steven Lehl, John McClelland Jr., Robin Patterson, and Karl Krey, who loaned photographs from their personal collections for use in the book and exhibit.

From first contact, the University of Washington Press immediately grasped the project's significance. Pat Soden and Marilyn Trueblood gave guidance and encouragement throughout the book's evolution. How fortunate to have the design talent of Ashley Saleeba who helped make this a book of beauty. Thanks as well to Christina Orange Dubois for her fine editing contributions and to Chris Beers, Richard Whitney, and Don McPhail, and Chuck Peven for their help with identifying historic fish distributions.

My unending gratitude and love go to my life partner, Susan Evans, and our wonderful children, Nathan and Genevieve, for supporting me while I jumped into the waters of this work. Finally, my appreciation and thanks go to friends for river trips of high adventure; to the Lost River People of Kettle Falls; to people who have welcomed me into their homes during research trips along the river; to Harold and Margaret Weed; and to my community, which for twenty-five years has faithfully stood by the river and this work.

Salmon Catch at Kettle Falls

Ellis Morigeau   William Teakle Collection, Northwest Room, Spokane Public Library

Library of Congress Cataloging-in-Publication Data

Layman, William D., 1946–
River of memory : the everlasting Columbia /
William D. Layman.— 1st ed.
p. cm.
ISBN 0-295-98591-7 (hardback : alk. paper)
ISBN 0-295-98592-5 (pbk. : alk. paper)

1. Columbia River—History—Pictorial works.
I. Title.
F853.L665   2006
979.7–dc22   2005028643

Library and Archives Canada Cataloguing in Publication

Layman, William D., 1946–
River of memory : the everlasting Columbia /
William D. Layman.

Includes bibliographical references and index.
ISBN-13: 978-0-7748-1303-7
ISBN-10: 0-7748-1303-2

1. Columbia River—History—Pictorial works.
2. Columbia River—History. I. Title.
F853.L39   2006   979.7'0022'2   C2005-906989-9